S. HRG. 115–180

SAFEGUARDING TO THE SEVENTH GENERATION: PROTECTION AND JUSTICE FOR INDIAN CHILDREN AND THE IMPLEMENTATION OF THE NATIVE AMERICAN CHILDREN'S SAFETY ACT OF 2016

FIELD HEARING

BEFORE THE

COMMITTEE ON INDIAN AFFAIRS
UNITED STATES SENATE

ONE HUNDRED FIFTEENTH CONGRESS

FIRST SESSION

APRIL 21, 2017

Printed for the use of the Committee on Indian Affairs

U.S. GOVERNMENT PUBLISHING OFFICE

28–892 PDF   WASHINGTON : 2018

For sale by the Superintendent of Documents, U.S. Government Publishing Office
Internet: bookstore.gpo.gov Phone: toll free (866) 512–1800; DC area (202) 512–1800
Fax: (202) 512–2104 Mail: Stop IDCC, Washington, DC 20402–0001

CONTENTS

SAFEGUARDING TO THE SEVENTH GENERATION: PROTECTION AND JUSTICE FOR INDIAN CHILDREN AND THE IMPLEMENTATION OF THE NATIVE AMERICAN CHILDREN'S SAFETY ACT OF 2016

FRIDAY, APRIL 21, 2017

U.S. SENATE,
COMMITTEE ON INDIAN AFFAIRS,
Fort Totten, ND.

The Committee met, pursuant to notice, at 1 p.m in the Cankdeska Cikana Community College Auditorium, Hon. John Hoeven, Chairman of the Committee, presiding.

OPENING STATEMENT OF HON. JOHN HOEVEN, U.S. SENATOR FROM NORTH DAKOTA

Senator HOEVEN. Good afternoon. Now, we'll call this hearing to order. And I want to thank Mr. Greg Holy Bull for the prayer and to the singers for the Drum Song.

And, of course, to the Honor Guard, both for the Flag Ceremony but even more for their service to our county. We appreciate them so much.

And I will remark right at the outset that, on a per capita basis, our Native American population, I believe, has a higher percentage of service in our military than any other group.

So that is really a remarkable and wonderful service to our country. So thank you so much to our veterans.

And also, I want to thank both President McDonald and Cynthia for hosting us here at this beautiful tribal college. And I appreciate so much your wonderful hospitality.

And President McDonald from the president of United Tribes Technical College, but Cynthia is from the school here. Thank you so much for hosting us. We appreciate it very much.

And also, I see that we have our Indian Affairs Commissioner here from Bismarck, Mr. Scott Davis.

And I'm not sure who appointed you originally, Scott. But whoever it was, if you see them, commend them for me, because I think you do a great job because you've served so well and continue to serve so well. And thank you for being here.

With that, I call this hearing to order. Today, the Committee will hold an oversight hearing on "Safeguarding to the Seventh Generation: Protection and Justice for Indian Children and Implementation of the Native American Children's Safety Act of 2016."

And I want to welcome everyone to this important hearing. And again, our thanks to Mr. Holy Bull and to the performers in the Honor Guard.

This is the first field hearing of the Senate Committee on Indian Affairs since I took over as chairman.

It's timely in coming to the Spirit Lake Indian Reservation. I understand that 2017 marks the 150th Anniversary of the Treaty of 1867.

This treaty was between the Federal Government and the Sisseton, Wahpeton, and Cut Head Bands of Yanktonais established the Spirit Lake Indian Reservation.

This treaty and anniversary reminds us of the long-standing relationship between the United States and the Spirit Lake Nation.

And today, we have an opportunity to forge a path forward to bring about a brighter future for our young people.

Native youth are two and a half times more likely to experience incidents involving child abuse or neglect than children of any other race or ethnicity. This figure is alarming and unacceptable.

It is also deeply troubling that placement in foster care of the child could also lead to that child's further involvement into the juvenile and criminal justice systems later in life. We need to break that cycle.

On June 14, the Administration for Children and Families published a report providing a framework of recommendations for improving the Spirit Lake Social Services programs.

I look forward to hearing a status update on those recommendations and how they've helped the children at the Spirit Lake Reservation.

We need to start turning the cycle of foster care to juvenile delinquency to prison around.

This is something that we see across the United States, and it's a current concern both on-reservation and off the reservation.

The title of the hearing is based on Tribal wisdom that we consider the effects of our decisions upon the protection, safety, and well-being of the children seven generations from now.

With this in mind, the Committee will examine how the Native American Children's Safety Act of 2016 is being implemented; what else could be done to improve the lives of children in this and other Native communities; and how other Indian communities can benefit from these efforts.

I introduced the Native American Children's Safety Act of 2016 last Congress as a step towards safer environments for Indian children.

It was signed into law on June 3, 2016. Among other things, this legislation expanded background check requirements for all adults residing in a prospective foster care home or facility. And of course, this applies across the entire country and all reservations.

The legislation also calls for the Department of the Interior to consult with Tribes and issue guidance regarding procedures for criminal records checks. These requirements are intended to lead to safer foster care homes for our children.

Tribal leaders and members over the years have consistently stressed their desire to help Native youth and make sure that they have every opportunity to succeed and remain in-touch with their tribal communities, traditions, and customs.

Safe and secure foster placement on the reservation is an important step in accomplishing that.

More active Tribal involvement in juvenile justice systems is also an important step.

My Indian Affairs staff is working with Senator Grassley and Representative Fox from North Carolina who chairs the Education and Workforce Committee on behalf of the House of Representatives on improving juvenile justice provisions in the Reauthorization of the Juvenile Justice and Delinquency Prevention Act.

These improvements and the fundamental requirements of the Native American Children's Safety Act of 2016, when implemented as intended, will enable this Act to accomplish more than just safe foster care homes.

I realize it's been a long journey towards finding solutions to build better lives for our children.

I want to thank the Council and staff from Tribal Social Services and Tribal Court, Tribal Victims Assistance Program, the BIA, and others who have worked to place Native youth on the Spirit Lake Reservation in a position to succeed.

There is still much work to be done, and I look forward to the testimony of our witnesses today. And so, we will hear from them.

We have with us Mr. Mike Black, who is the acting secretary for Indian Affairs—Bureau of Indian Affairs, U.S. Department of the Interior, Washington, D.C.

Nikki Hatch, regional administrator for the Administration for Children and Families, U.S. Department of Health and Human Services, in Washington, D.C.

We have the Honorable Myra Pearson, Tribal Chairperson, Spirit Lake Nation. Thank you for being here.

And, of course, Dr. Cynthia Lindquist, president of Cankdeska Cikana Community College, and our host today. Again, thank you for hosting. I appreciate it so much.

And to all of you, we appreciate that you are here for your testimony and also to answer questions.

I want to remind you that your full written testimony will be made part of the official record, and we'll begin with your opening statements.

I also want to take a moment to thank my Committee staff for being here, as well as members of my personal staff, as well as Representative Cramer's staff for being here to join us, as well.

Thank you for being here. We appreciate it very much—as well as all others here, gathered. So with that, I will turn to our witnesses and begin with Mr. Michael Black.

STATEMENT OF MICHAEL S. BLACK, ACTING ASSISTANT SECRETARY—INDIAN AFFAIRS, U.S. DEPARTMENT OF THE INTERIOR

Mr. BLACK. Good afternoon, Chairman Hoeven. And again, my name is Michael Black. I am currently the acting assistant secretary for Indian Affairs in the Department of the Interior.

Thank you for the opportunity to present testimony for the Department of the Interior on the "Safeguarding to the Seventh Generation: Protection and Justice for Indian Children and the Implementation of the Native American Children's Safety Act of 2016."

The safety of Native children is a priority for Indian Affairs and the Department. The Bureau of Indian Affairs' Human Services and BIA Public Safety and Justice programs support Native American families and communities and address the significant challenges faced by children throughout Indian Country.

The Native American Children's Safety Act of 2016 addresses the need for Tribal Social Services agencies to conduct comprehensive background checks of residents in foster homes and employees of foster care institutions before placing children in foster care.

It expands the Indian Child Protection and Family Violence Prevention Act of 1990, which required character investigations of federal and Tribal employees who had regular contact with or control over Indian children.

The Act also requires complete criminal background records checks on every covered individual who resides in the household or who is employed at the institution in which the foster care placement will be made.

Additionally, the Act requires Tribes to establish standards of placement that include a criminal records check, including fingerprint-based checks of national crime information databases; a check of any abuse registries maintained by the Tribe; and a check of any child abuse and neglect registry maintained by the state in which the covered individual resides or previously resided in the previous five years.

The Act also requires that the Department consult with Tribes and issue guidance regarding these procedures.

In preparation for developing this guidance, the BIA is currently in the process of identifying best practices of social service agencies in Indian Country, with a view toward how they can be adapted for use by social services agencies.

As an example, at the Fort Totten Agency serving the Spirit Lake Tribe, the BIA conducts background checks on all relative placements either prior to placement or in conjunction with emergency placements.

There are three levels of checks conducted by BIA to ensure the safety of Indian children, and we believe it is a best practice model that can be replicated nationwide.

The first check is a tribal name-based check, which is completed immediately in the case of an emergency placement.

The Fort Totten Agency then calls the BIA Office of Justice Services to request a name-based background check on all individuals residing in a home prior to the emergency placement of a child.

Within 24 hours prior to granting care and control of a child, the Agency conducts a background check of state criminal records through a search of the State of North Dakota website.

Finally, all relative placements undergo a full federal background check in which the Fort Totten Agency takes the individuals' fingerprints and sends them to a third-party vendor under contract with BIA that carries out that review.

The Agency typically receives the results of the background checks back within a week.

The BIA is also examining processes that will provide the Tribes the ability to check child abuse and neglect registries maintained by the state.

Such processes will require cooperation of state governments, and we look forward to continuing developing these relationships.

As mentioned above, the BIA is required to consult on the required guidance, and we expect to begin those consultations in the fall of 2017.

Thank you again for the opportunity to testify on this very important issue: The Protection and Justice for Indian Children and the Implementation of the Native American Children's Safety Act of 2016.

The Department is committed to doing its part to ensure the safety and protection of children throughout Indian Country. I will be glad to answer any questions the Committee may have. Thank you very much.

[The prepared statement of Mr. Black follows:]

PREPARED STATEMENT OF MICHAEL S. BLACK, ACTING ASSISTANT SECRETARY—
INDIAN AFFAIRS, U.S. DEPARTMENT OF THE INTERIOR

Chairman Hoeven, my name is Michael Black and I am the Acting Assistant Secretary for Indian Affairs at the Department of the Interior. Thank you for the opportunity to present testimony for the Department of the Interior (Department) on, "Safeguarding to the Seventh Generation: Protection and Justice for Indian Children and the Implementation of the Native American Children's Safety Act of 2016."

The safety of Native children is a Departmental priority. The Bureau of Indian Affairs' (BIA) Human Services and BIA Public Safety and Justice programs support Native American families and communities and address the significant challenges faced by children throughout Indian Country.

The Native American Children's Safety Act of 2016 (NACSA) addresses the need for tribal social services agencies to conduct comprehensive background checks of residents in foster homes and employees of foster care institutions before placing children in foster care. In this way, the Act expands the Indian Child Protection and Family Violence Prevention Act of 1990, which required character investigations of federal and tribal employees who had regular contact with or control over Indian children.

The NACSA requires that, prior to finalizing a foster care placement, the tribal social services agency must complete a criminal records check on every covered individual who resides in the household or is employed at the institution in which the foster care placement will be made. Additionally, the Act requires Tribes to establish standards of placement that include: a criminal records check, including fingerprint-based checks of national crime information databases; a check of any abuse registries maintained by the Tribe; and a check of any child abuse and neglect registry maintained by the State in which the covered individual resides or previously resided in the preceding five years. The NACSA also requires that the Department consult with Tribes and issue guidance regarding these procedures.

In preparation for developing this guidance, the BIA is currently in the process of identifying best practices of social service agencies in Indian Country, with a view toward how they can be adapted for use by tribal social services agencies. As an example, at the Fort Totten Agency serving the Spirit Lake Tribe, the BIA conducts background checks on all relative placements either prior to placement or in conjunction with emergency placements. There are three levels of checks conducted by BIA to ensure the safety of Indian children and we believe it is a best practices model that can be replicated nationwide.

The first check is a tribal name based check, which is completed immediately in the case of an emergency placement. The Fort Totten Agency then calls the BIA-Office of Justice Services to request a name-based background check on all individuals residing in a home prior to the emergency placement of a child. Within 24 hours prior to granting care and control of a child, the Agency conducts a background check of state criminal records through a search of the State of North Dakota website. Finally, all relative placements undergo a full federal background check in which the Fort Totten Agency takes the individuals' fingerprints and sends them to a third party vendor under contract with the BIA that carries out that review. The Agency typically receives the results of the background check within a week.

The BIA is also examining processes that will provide Tribes the ability to check child abuse and neglect registries maintained by States. Such processes will require the cooperation of State governments, and we look forward to continue developing those relationships. As mentioned above, the BIA is required to consult on the required guidance and we expect to begin consultations in the fall of 2017.

Conclusion

Thank you for the opportunity to testify on the issue, "Protection and Justice for Indian Children and the Implementation of the Native American Children's Safety Act of 2016." The Department is committed to doing its part to ensure the safety and protection of children throughout Indian Country. I would be glad to answer any questions the Committee may have.

Senator HOEVEN. Thank you, Secretary. I appreciate it. And now, Ms. Nikki Hatch.

STATEMENT OF NIKKI HATCH, REGIONAL ADMINISTRATOR, ADMINISTRATION FOR CHILDREN AND FAMILIES, REGION 8, U.S. DEPARTMENT OF HEALTH AND HUMAN SERVICES

Ms. HATCH. Thank you, Chairman Hoeven. It's my honor to appear before this Committee on behalf of the Department of Health and Human Services.

My name is Nikki Hatch. I'm a regional administrator for the Administration for Children and Families in Region 8.

As regional administrator, I partner with State, local, community-based organizations, and Tribes within the region to promote economic and social well-being of children, families, individuals, and communities.

My testimony today will focus on ACF programs that support Indian child welfare, our support of the child welfare community at the Spirit Lake Reservation, and our work related to the Native American Children's Safety Act of 2016.

Within ACF, the Children's Bureau oversees funding related to child abuse and neglect prevention and intervention, which include addressing trauma; family preservation; foster care; adoption; and guardianship.

Today, many Tribes operate some form of Child Protection Services, and many have tribal codes; court systems; and child welfare programs.

Historically, Tribes have accessed much of their child welfare funding through the States or through the BIA.

However, the Children's Bureau also offers direct funding opportunities for Tribes through several grant programs which were made available to Tribes through the Fostering Connections Act of 2008.

For example, the Fostering Connections Act authorized one-time grants of up to $300,000 to Tribes to assist in the development of a tribally operated title IV–E plan. Over the past seven years, 35 Tribes or consortia of Tribes have received such grants.

Under the Stephanie Tubbs Jones Child Welfare Services Program, funds are also available to Tribes to improve their child welfare services with the goal of keeping families together.

In fiscal year 2016, 186 Tribes received approximately $6.4 million in program funds. Funds are also available for certain eligible Tribes under the Promoting Safe and Stable Families Program to assist with family support, family preservation services, time-limited family reunification services, and services to support adoptions.

In fiscal year 2016, 130 Tribes received approximately $10.3 million in those program funds.

The Spirit Lake Tribe is a recipient of some of the program funds I've mentioned. The Tribe is a title IV–B grantee and receives title IV–E dollars through an agreement with the State of North Dakota.

In addition to funding, Spirit Lake has access to the ACF Capacity-Building Center for Tribes.

This Center delivers services to Tribal communities through coaching, peer networking, distance learning, consultation, dissemination, product development, and capacity-building assistance.

Over the years, we've worked directly with child welfare stakeholders at the Spirit Lake Reservation to provide a foundation and framework to support practice improvement efforts within Spirit Lake's child welfare program.

For example, in response to a number of concerns shared with us by the community, including concerns that children reported for abuse and neglect were placed and remained in unsafe conditions, ACF representatives held on-site listening sessions at the Spirit Lake Reservation in 2014.

The sessions included interviews with a range of Spirit Lake child welfare stakeholders. Based on those sessions, we developed seven priority recommendations to be addressed by child welfare stakeholders at the Spirit Lake Reservation.

Included was a recommendation for the Spirit Lake Tribal Social Services Agency and BIA to jointly develop policies and procedures that encompass all aspects of child welfare services, including that foster homes must comply with federal and state safety checks, including background checks on all adults residing in the home.

In 2016, the Native American Children's Safety Act addressed background check requirements for foster homes.

As you know, the law set new standards and requirements for Tribes operating programs under the Department of the Interior to implement background checks for Tribal foster family homes to ensure the safety of children.

In addition to the Act's requirement, Tribes that receive funding through title IV–E and title IV–B for child welfare programs are required to license foster family homes and child care institutions and conduct criminal and child abuse background checks.

As the licensing and background check requirements for foster care placements may be different under both laws, we're working with Tribes to ensure that HHS program requirements are clear.

We also continue to support the Department of the Interior's efforts to implement the licensing and background check requirements of the Native American Children's Safety Act.

Thank you for your commitment to the safety and well-being of Indian children. I look forward to working with you on continuing to find ways to improve services provided in tribal communities and to ensure the safety of Native American children, and I'd be happy to answer any questions.

[The prepared statement of Ms. Hatch follows:]

PREPARED STATEMENT OF NIKKI HATCH, REGIONAL ADMINISTRATOR, ADMINISTRATION FOR CHILDREN AND FAMILIES, REGION 8, U.S. DEPARTMENT OF HEALTH AND HUMAN SERVICES

Chairman Hoeven, Vice Chairman Udall, and members of the Committee, it is my honor to appear before this Committee on behalf of the Department of Health and Human Services (HHS). I am Nikki Hatch, Regional Administrator for the Administration for Children and Families (ACF), Region 8, which serves Colorado, Montana, North Dakota, South Dakota, Utah, and Wyoming. As Regional Administrator, I partner with state, local, community-based organizations, and tribes within the region to promote economic and social well-being of children, families, individuals, and communities.

ACF is a committed partner with agencies across the federal family, including with the Department of Interior's Bureau of Indian Affairs (BIA), and with tribes. We work with partners to protect the best interests of Indian youth and children, and promote the stability and security of Indian tribes and families.

My testimony today will focus on ACF programs that support Indian child welfare, our support of the child welfare community at the Spirit Lake Reservation, and our work related to the Native American Children's Safety Act of 2016.

Children's Bureau Grants to Tribes

Within ACF, the Children's Bureau oversees funding related to child abuse and neglect prevention and intervention which include addressing trauma, family preservation, foster care, adoption, and guardianship.

Today, many tribes operate some form of child protection services and many have tribal codes, court systems, and child welfare programs. Historically, tribes have accessed much of their child welfare funding through the states, or through the BIA. However, the Children's Bureau also offers direct funding opportunities for tribes through several grant programs.

The Fostering Connections to Success and Increasing Adoptions Act of 2008 amended title IV–E of the Social Security Act, and provided federally-recognized Indian tribes, tribal organizations or consortia of Indian tribes with the option to apply to operate a title IV–E program and seek federal reimbursement for a share of allowable expenditures made pursuant to an approved title IV–E plan for foster care, guardianship assistance, and adoption assistance for children with special needs. Since passage of the law, nine tribes have been approved to operate a title IV–E program. These are:

- Port Gamble S'Klallam Tribe of Kingston, Washington;
- Confederated Salish and Kootenai Tribes of Pablo, Montana;
- South Puget Intertribal Planning Agency of Shelton, Washington;
- Keweenaw Bay Indian Community, Baraga, Michigan;
- Navajo Nation, Window Rock, Arizona;
- Chickasaw Nation, Ada, Oklahoma;
- Eastern Band of Cherokee Indians, Cherokee, North Carolina;
- Pascua Yaqui Tribe, Tucson, Arizona; and
- Tolowa Dee-ni' Nation (formerly Smith River Rancheria) in California.

Seven of the tribes are moving forward with implementation of their title IV–E programs, while two have chosen not to move forward at this time.

The Fostering Connections Act also authorized one-time grants of up to $300,000 to tribes, to assist in the development of a tribally operated title IV–E plan. Grant funds may be used for the cost of developing a title IV–E plan, including costs for the development of data collection systems, a cost allocation methodology, agency and tribal court procedures necessary to meet the case review system requirements, or any other costs attributable to meeting any other requirement necessary for approval of a title IV–E plan. Over the past seven years, 35 tribes or consortia of tribes have received title IV–E plan development grants.

The Fostering Connections Act also provided both tribes that operate a title IV–E program and tribes that have a title IV–E cooperative agreement or contract with the state title IV–E agency, the option to apply to receive funds directly from HHS to operate a John H. Chafee Foster Care Independence (CFCIP) and/or Educational Training Voucher Program (ETV). The CFCIP and ETV programs provide funds to help older youth in foster care and youth formerly in foster care acquire training and independent living skills and attend postsecondary education so they can become self-sufficient. In fiscal year (FY) 2016, four tribes received approximately $100,000 in funds through the CFCIP and ETV programs.

Additional funds, under the Stephanie Tubbs Jones Child Welfare Services Program (Subpart 1 of title IV–B of the Social Security Act), are available to tribes to improve their child welfare services with the goal of keeping families together. Tribes provide services in support of five purposes which are: protecting and promoting the welfare of all children; preventing the neglect, abuse, or exploitation of children; supporting at-risk families through services which allow children, where appropriate, to remain safely with their families or return to their families in a timely manner; promoting the safety, permanence, and well-being of children in foster care and adoptive families; and finally, providing training, professional development and support to ensure a well-qualified child welfare workforce. In FY 2016, 186 tribes received approximately $6.4 million in funds through the program.

Funds are also available for certain eligible tribes under the Promoting Safe and Stable Families Program (Subpart 2 of title IV–B of the Social Security Act) to assist with family support, family preservation services, time-limited family reunification services, and services to support adoptions. In FY 2016, 130 tribes received approximately $10.3 million in funds under title IV–B, subpart 2.

In 2011, the Child and Family Services Improvement and Innovation Act allocated $1 million for the creation of new Tribal Court Improvement Program (CIP) grants. The purpose of the grants is to design and implement projects and/or activities to assess, expand, or enhance the effectiveness of tribal courts and/or legal representation in cases related to child welfare, family preservation, family reunification, guardianship, and adoption. Tribes and tribal consortia are eligible to compete for this grant if they: (1) operate a title IV–E program; or (2) plan to operate a title IV–E program and have received a title IV–E plan development grant; or (3) have a court responsible for proceedings related to foster care or adoption. There have been two rounds of grants under this program, with seven awards in the first round, and nine awards in the second. The second three-year grant began in FY 2015, with each grantee receiving up to $150,000 for each of three years. Current grantees include:

- Confederated Salish and Kootenai Tribes;
- Muckleshoot Indian Tribe;
- Ponca Tribe of Nebraska;
- Citizen Potawatomi Nation;
- Mashpee Wampanoag;
- Taos Pueblo;
- Sitka Tribe of Alaska;
- Saint Regis Mohawk Tribe; and,
- Tolowa Dee-ni' Nation (formerly Smith River Rancheria).

ACF and the Spirit Lake Child Welfare Community

The Spirit Lake Tribe is a title IV–B grantee and receives title IV–E dollars through an agreement with the State of North Dakota. As a title IV–B grantee, Spirit Lake has access to the ACF Capacity Building Collaborative, which is composed of three highly integrated centers to serve tribes, states territories, and courts. The Capacity Building Center for Tribes delivers services to tribal communities through coaching, peer networking, distance learning, consultation, dissemination, product development, and capacity-building assistance.

We have worked directly with child welfare stakeholders at the Spirit Lake Reservation to provide a foundation and framework to support practice improvement efforts within Spirit Lake's child welfare program. For example, in response to a number of concerns shared with us by the community, including concerns that children reported for abuse and neglect were placed and remained in unsafe conditions, ACF representatives held on-site listening sessions at the Spirit Lake Reservation in 2014. The sessions included interviews with a range of stakeholders from the Spirit Lake Tribal child welfare system, including current and former social workers, current and former juvenile judges, BIA staff, school district staff, North Dakota and county human services staff, and BIA law enforcement.

Based on those listening sessions, we developed seven priority recommendations to be addressed by child welfare stakeholders at the Spirit Lake Reservation. Included was a recommendation for the Spirit Lake Tribal Social Services Agency and BIA to jointly develop policies and procedures that encompass all aspects of child welfare services including that foster homes must comply with federal and state safety checks, including background checks on all adults residing in the home.

The Native American Children's Safety Act of 2016

The Native American Children's Safety Act of 2016 set new standards and requirements for tribes operating programs under the Department of Interior to implement background checks for tribal foster family homes to ensure the safety of children. In addition, tribes that receive funding through titles IV–E and IV–B for child welfare programs are required to license foster family homes and child care institutions and conduct criminal and child abuse background checks. As the licensing and background check requirements for foster care placements are slightly different under both laws, we are working with tribes to ensure the title IV–E requirements are clear. We also continue to support the Department of Interior in its efforts to implement the licensing and background check requirements of the Native American Children's Safety Act.

Thank you for your commitment to the safety and well-being of Indian children. I look forward to working with you on continuing to find ways to improve services provided in tribal communities and to ensure the safety of Native American children. I would be happy to answer any questions.

Senator HOEVEN. Thank you, Administrator. And now, Chairwoman Myra Pearson.

STATEMENT OF HON. MYRA PEARSON, CHAIRWOMAN, SPIRIT LAKE TRIBE

Ms. PEARSON. Thank you, Chairman Hoeven, for this opportunity. And I also appreciate the fact that my comments will be a part of the record today. I thank you for that.

The Spirit Lake Tribe has struggled to develop a sustainable, systematic infrastructure to address child deprivation within the Spirit Lake Tribe jurisdiction.

The obstacles and challenges that the Tribe has faced Stem, in part, from the Bureau of Indian Affairs'—hereinafter, the BIA—regulations that hinder information-sharing and Tribal justice system responses; burdensome foster care licensing standards and requirements that limit the availability of licensed foster care homes on the Spirit Lake Reservation; and a lack of necessary resources to build a justice system response to child deprivation that is effective, sustainable, and culturally appropriate.

Presently, the Spirit Lake Tribe is working diligently to reassume control of Child Protective Services through the 638 contracting process.

As a part of that effort, the Spirit Lake Tribe is updating applicable policies, procedures, and laws.

The Spirit Lake Tribe has filed our Letter of Intent with the United States Department of the Interior, and we are working to identify costs while further negotiating a base level of funding for our Child Protective Services division.

The process has been frustrated by BIA's unwillingness to provide case-related information and to work with the Tribal justice system personnel.

The communication break-downs between the BIA and the Spirit Lake Tribe regarding Child Protective Services have directly impacted the safety of our children.

Despite the fact that the Tribe intends to reassume control of Child Protective Services, the BIA has made it clear that the funding to the Tribe will be significantly less than the current BIA budget.

In other words, the BIA is seemingly content to turn the Child Protective Services function over to the Tribe through the 638 Contract process, but it is clear that we will be expected to provide the same or better services with less funding and less personnel.

This hardly appears to be a recipe for success, and one that we will continue to address through the negotiation process.

The Spirit Lake Tribe also works cooperatively with the State of North Dakota to meet the needs of children on the Spirit Lake Reservation through a title IV–E agreement.

In accordance with that agreement, the Spirit Lake Tribe agrees to follow the applicable title IV–E law and regulations.

And so far, as the Title IV–E Agreement law and regulations pertain to foster care and foster care licensing, the Title IV–E Agreement includes in relevant part.

Title IV–E-reimbursed maintenance payments may only be made to licensed or approved foster care home facilities, and the Spirit Lake Tribe is responsible to license such homes or facilities on the Reservation, subject to departmental recognition of the licensure by the Tribe of any foster home or facility on or near the Reservation, in accordance with the adoption of the Safe Families Act and implementing regulations.

The regulations may be found in 45 CFR 11355.20, Part A. The process for the foster home licensure for the Spirit Lake Tribe begins through a receipt of a referral form or direct application by a home wanting to be licensed.

Upon receipt of these forms, the process of becoming an adoptive or foster parent begins. The process of licensure is oftentimes time-consuming.

The licensure process can take anywhere from a few months to a year to complete. This timeframe includes the submission of an application, completion of a home study, training, and completion of necessary criminal background checks.

To ensure that there are systematic checks and balances in place for the foster care licensing process on the Spirit Lake Reservation, the Spirit Lake Tribal Welfare Committee conducts final screenings and recommendations based upon an established checklist.

Despite the existence of the checklist, we are finding that many applications for foster care licensure are incomplete, as they are void of such essential information as criminal background checks.

In order for a home to be licensed for foster care on the Spirit Lake Reservation, an applicant must meet minimum requirements; submit all required forms and information; complete the required criminal background checks; and submit fingerprints for all household members that are 18 years of age and over.

Despite the obstacles we have encountered regarding Child Protective Services, the Spirit Lake Tribe continues to develop our Tribal Social Services program.

In recent years, the Tribe has participated in the Tiwahe Initiative; developed guiding principles for the program; increased web-based information and resources; and provided community-wide education and culturally relevant training.

The Spirit Lake Tribal Social Services Program also provides foster home recruitment, licensing, and support services.

These efforts include locating families interested in providing foster care, conducting home studies, and assisting with the coordination of training.

Our over-arching goal is to continue to improve the overall Tribal justice system responses to child deprivation cases on the Spirit Lake Reservation.

This begins by increasing local autonomy to design a systematic response that is viable; sustainable; and, more importantly, that meets the needs of the children and families being served.

In order to realize our goal, it is imperative that we have necessary resources. The number one obstacle or challenge that we face as a Tribe in developing sustainable and effective responses to child deprivation matters on the Spirit Lake Reservation is a lack of essential resources.

The lack of sufficient funding to support Child Protective Services resulted in the Tribe turning that function back to the BIA a few years ago.

However, since that time, a systematic assessment has been brought to light of even greater resource deficiencies.

The resource deficiencies go far beyond Child Protective Services and reach into our child welfare system, court system, and post-adjudication services.

Among the resource deficiencies that we have identified include personnel shortages within Child Protective Services; personnel shortages within child welfare case management; insufficient funding to support ongoing training needs for the Tribal Social Services personnel and Tribal justice system personnel responsible for addressing child deprivation cases; lack of local resources to support the development of culturally appropriate services for court-involved families; and lack of physical infrastructure to accommodate Tribal Social Services personnel while providing a space for the delivery of services to the families.

Our program currently operates out of a decade-old mobile home. The lack of aforementioned resources significantly hinders our ability as a Tribe to maintain appropriate case file management ratios, develop meaningful case plans, and facilitate reunification efforts.

Furthermore, our rural location; inadequate office space; lack of access to affordable on-reservation housing; and historically low funding levels have made it very difficult for the Spirit Lake Tribal Social Services program to attract competent professionals to fill position vacancies within Child Protective Services and Tribal social service divisions.

I am convinced that the Spirit Lake Tribe would be better able to protect and safeguard our children were the resource deficiencies noted above remedied.

By meeting the needs of our Spirit Lake Tribal Social Services program through adequate physical infrastructure, personnel, staff training, and culturally relevant services, we would not only be equipped to respond to incidents of child deprivation, but we would also be able to focus efforts on prevention, as well.

Thank you for your consideration of these comments and for considering how the United States government might work with us in the spirit of Tribal self-determination as we work towards safeguarding our children and our larger community. Thank you, and I will be open for questions. Thank you.

Senator HOEVEN. Thank you, Chairwoman. Dr. Lindquist.

STATEMENT OF CYNTHIA LINDQUIST, Ph.D., PRESIDENT, CANKDESKA CIKANA COMMUNITY COLLEGE, SPIRIT LAKE DAKOTA NATION

Dr. LINDQUIST. My name is Cynthia Lindquist: President, Cankdeska Cikana Community College; Tribal member, Spirit Lake Dakota Nation, Fort Totten, North Dakota.

Thank you, Senator Hoeven and your staff, for the opportunity and the privilege of hosting the field hearing for the United States Senate Committee on Indian Affairs. I am honored to be here and to have been asked to present and to speak.

Dakota people do not have a word for "child." My grandmas and grandpas, my elders, have taught me that we call our little ones "Wakanheza," sacred little ones.

It's important to acknowledge the cultural component to calling the little ones "sacred."

Your hearing today is about the implementation of an Act toward the protection, the safety, the well-being of Native children.

I believe this Act and the actions of this Committee will bring forward light and information; data. More importantly, I am ever-hopeful that the work of this Committee will bring action.

There are many issues related to child protection, child safety. These are interrelated, interconnected. And there is no one solution; it's complicated.

And yet, for me, as a president of a college, as a grandma, and as our Chairwoman has eloquently stated, we need a significant infusion of resources.

The issues are complex, they are layered, and they are interwoven. I am very hopeful that this Act, again, will shed light and bring action and attention and resources.

Some aspects of this is disappointing that, in today's world, we have to have such an Act to protect Indian children, Indian babies.

We have come this far based on history; historical trauma; complex policies and programs and services.

The needs for Native people, for reservation communities, are complex and related to these things. They are rooted in and compounded by endemic poverty.

This complexity has led and taught our people to be dependent. And so, the whole philosophical aspect of breaking dependencies is taking much work.

And yet, we have a lot of pieces of that picture, of that system, in place: The industriousness, the ingenuity and compassion, the generosity, the resiliency of Indigenous people and Dakota people is prevalent. We are here today to share that; to share the story; to be part of it.

In 2015, Cankdeska Cikana Community College, along with the Spirit Lake Dakota Nation, commissioned a comprehensive community assessment. I have noted this in my formal written testimony.

We have a link to the College website. There are three documents: The full report itself is about 180 pages; there's an executive summary that's about 4 pages long; we also commissioned a cultural narrative to complement this comprehensive community assessment.

In this assessment is a plethora of data from various sources: The Bureau of Indian Affairs, the Administration for Children and

Families, the United States Census, the Indian Health Service, the Department of Public Instruction.

There are data; there are reports and documents abounding, in abundancy, that everyone has access to. I just want to highlight a couple of data points that is in my testimony, again.

The median age of our people on this reservation is 23.4, compared to the state's median age of 37, or the nation's median age of 37.2.

Twenty-seven percent of our people, of our population on this Reservation, is under the age of 19.

Fifty-seven percent of our children live in poverty on this Reservation. Benson County has almost double the U.S. poverty rate of 14 percent, and it's close to 30 percent for the Spirit Lake Dakota and Benson County.

Most all the Native children in the school systems for the Lake Region and there are five (5) high schools that feed Cankdeska Cikana Community College, but 75 to 80 percent of those children are eligible for reduced and free meals.

This, again, this data, these numbers play into this dependency lifestyle. And when we're talking about the protection of children, the safety of children, we have to be cognizant of these things.

But again, there's data; there's reports. In this comprehensive community assessment—and I have copies out there, in addition to having access on our website—the people of this reservation cited the number one need: Child protection; child safety; the health and well-being of our children.

Respondents want more services; local services; better-quality services that are available locally.

They want more planned activities for children and youth, particularly activities that will focus on the issue of substance abuse and address youth risk factors for drug and alcohol use.

Our people want coordinated care. They would also like to be served by Native professionals, trained Native professionals, in all gamuts, in all systems that provide these services, be it child protection; law enforcement; social services; healthcare; education; the whole gamut of what is needed out here.

We need a coordinated plan of action toward resource development that puts the agencies together to better put those pots of money together to reach our people at the local level so that these services, these resources are accessible to Tribal programs; Tribal leaders; the Tribal College; the Tribal court system; Tribal Social Services.

Included in that resource development has to be the emphasis and priority of education: The training and the development of professionals for all of these disciplines.

Homes: We're talking about helping families. If our families don't have homes, if our families are hungry, if our families are worried about Pampers or milk for baby, it's hard to talk to them about education; or a sense of health and well-being; or child services, and being a better parent.

Our community needs facilities, and we need rec facilities that are appropriate for the North Dakota weather and our geographic location. We need these services to be integrated and coordinated and available locally.

The Tribal College, Cankdeska Cikana Community College, manages, for the Tribe, the Head Start program.

Head Start is a wonderful model of services for people that emphasize children and the development of children.

We took over the management of the program in January of 2014. We serve about 140 children, infant to five years old.

We have a prenatal component to Head Start, wherein we have a couple of nurses who go out to try to provide prenatal care.

And if that mother comes in for services, they are guaranteed a slot in Head Start.

The few moments of time I have to visit with staff individually and personally about their jobs and their role, the nurse who does this prenatal service as part of our Head Start program has told me about the challenge of finding these young women.

And she was trained by my mother, fortunately, so she knows the Reservation well and knows how to find people.

So when we find these young women, they're reluctant to come. There is some shame, there is some hesitancy, because they're afraid of being punished; afraid of being denigrated if they're using, and that. Our goal in the program is to just find these women, to get them into services. So many times, these nurses and also our other social work staff within the Head Start program—they're called "FSA," family services advocates—they're sitting in the car on the Reservation, trying to counsel these young mothers to come into services.

They learned to have iPads, the technology, and a printer so they can do the intake; try to refer them to the Tribe's prenatal program to get them into services, and that.

It takes much work and time and much effort, but I cite this as an example. Head Start is also—along with us at the College, our programs, and what we do—we are a mandatory reporter for child abuse and neglect, or suspected cases of child abuse and neglect.

It's disheartening for me to have to report officially that, since January of 2017—so three and a half months—our Head Start program has submitted sixteen 960s to the Bureau of Indian Affairs Child Protection Program here in Fort Totten.

Our problem or our concern with this is that we feel, when we submit a 960, it goes into a big black hole because we don't hear back.

We don't know if they got the 960; we don't know if it's going to be acted upon or investigated. And our concern is for the children.

And so, then, every now and then, my staff will ask me, "Did you hear? Did anybody contact you, President?"

"No, and that's really not my job; not my role or function."

"Do you know if the child's okay? Is that family okay?"

At the same time, on occasion, we file a 960 with Ramsey County in Devils Lake, North Dakota.

And on the few occasions that that has happened, they've called us back in less than an hour to tell us, "I've received your 960. Yes, that's our client. We're going to investigate."

And then, typically, they'll ask a few more questions. So we know social services can work.

We know the reality of the Bureau of Indian Affairs Child Protection Program, and the complications of it being either Tribal Social Services or the Federal Government Bureau of Indian Affairs Social Services, and the staff coming and going as temporary assignments to this Reservation.

But I mention this and bring this up because, if we're really about protecting children, there is still much work to be done.

The College is building a new Head Start Center. We hope to open in August or September this fall.

The staff at Head Start and the community is very excited. This is a partnership between Cankdeska Cikana Community College and the Spirit Lake Dakota Nation and our Tribal Council.

It's a great example of working together to address this issue of facilities and services for our children and families.

I mention the building because we took out a loan which, it's like, Why did we have to take out a loan?

Benson County Spirit Lake Dakota Reservation is a Strike Force Zone; it's a Promise Zone.

And I'm very, very proud as a Tribal member that the College negotiated and facilitated taking out the loan.

There's two loans, actually, for $7.6 million. The Spirit Lake Dakota Tribal Council is making the payments for that loan.

And it's a true partnership. And I'm really, really proud of our Tribal leaders, and I wanted to acknowledge them publicly.

At the same time, they know, since we've signed those loan papers, we've been trying to get them changed; minimized; hardship-decreased; or something, surely.

Because, again, Spirit Lake Dakota Nation, Fort Totten, North Dakota: Can't something be done to decrease those loans? But we have started making the payments.

Another component or issue relative to Head Start that is reflected in all of this addresses children's issues is education and the need for training.

We're successful through the College in providing professional development, but we have much more work to do toward getting Tribal members with the appropriate credentials.

And the training is for teachers in early childhood education, elementary education, education in general; social workers, clinicians, forensic social workers who can do this work but who have the cultural sensitivity; we need multi-disciplinary teams.

I want to close by citing a comment out of the United Nations' report from 2009, The State of the World's Indigenous Peoples:

Education is the primary vehicle by which economically and socially marginalized people can lift themselves out of poverty and obtain a means to participate fully in their communities.

I'm a little biased as the president of a Tribal community college. Many of us have stories about how education has helped us.

And there's many types of education, especially for us as indigenous people. Unfortunately, it's not funded equitably; it's not funded adequately.

And that's a huge component of all of this and the solutions toward implementing this Act. I am most hopeful, but there is still much work to be done.

And hopefully, we will continue that journey together in a good way, not pointing fingers at anybody or any one thing.

How do we figure this out? I am most optimistic and hopeful. Thank you so much for the opportunity and for listening.

[The prepared statement of Dr. Lindquist follows:]

PREPARED STATEMENT OF CYNTHIA LINDQUIST, PH.D., PRESIDENT, CANKDESKA CIKANA COMMUNITY COLLEGE, SPIRIT LAKE DAKOTA NATION

Thank you to Senator John Hoeven and the U.S. Senate Committee on Indian Affairs for hosting a field hearing on the Spirit Lake Dakota reservation on the very important topic of child safety and protection. I believe this is the first time a Senate field hearing will be held on the Spirit Lake reservation, and I am grateful that our Senate leader has convened the hearing in Fort Totten, ND.

Dakota people do not have a word for child or kids as they are considered "sacred little ones"—wakanheza. Human life is sacred, a gift, and the sacred little ones are to be loved, cared for, and cherished. I am ever hopeful that the *Native American Children's Safety Act of 2016* will shed light on, and bring action to the layered, yet related issues to protect our sacred little ones. There is no one solution except for the need for significant infusion of resources—financial and professional—to address the safety and protection of Native children. While I am most hopeful for the potential benefit of the Act, it is also disheartening that such legislation is needed.

The needs for the Spirit Lake Dakota reservation are significant and documented in a variety of ways by various federal, state, and private organizations. Disparities in social, health, education, and economic factors are reported by the U.S. Census, Bureau of Indian Affairs, Indian Health Service, and many others. The needs for most reservation communities are complex, related to history and historical trauma, and compounded by endemic poverty. This complexity has forced Native people to live a dependency lifestyle that is alien to Dakota life ways of industriousness, ingenuity, compassion, and generosity.

In 2015, CCCC led the coordination of a Comprehensive Community Assessment (CCA) in partnership with the Spirit Lake Tribe. The purpose of the assessment was to describe community characteristics using existing data and to describe current health, education, economic, housing status, and needs of community members through individual interviews. There are three documents for the CCA—the full study/report, an executive summary, and a cultural narrative. These documents may be accessed on the CCCC web site at *http://www.littlehoop.edu/research.html*. The following demographic summary is from the CCA:

Spirit Lake Nation has 7,256 enrolled members with 2,069 members living on the reservation. Total reservation population is 4,238. The Department of Interior, Bureau of Indian Affairs, lists 5,002 American Indian/Alaska Natives (AI/AN) alone or in combination, living on or near the Spirit Lake Dakota reservation. Virtually the same number of females and males live on the reservation. The median age for all of Spirit Lake reservation is 23.4, younger than the State's median age of 37 or the nation's median age of 37.2. Women have a higher median age (23.5) than men (23.3). The reservation community has approximately 27 percent of the population under the age of 19. The reservation's 65 and older population comprises 7.1 percent of the total population, lower than the state (14.5 percent) and national (13 percent) percentages. Twenty-nine percent of Spirit Lake reservation residents are married, lower than the state (53.5 percent) and U.S. (50.2 percent).

According to the 2010 U.S. Census Bureau, 72 percent of Spirit Lake reservation residents, age 18 and older graduated from high school, as compared to ND at 89 percent and the U.S. at 85 percent. Spirit Lake Tribal members earning a bachelor's degree or higher is 7 percent, compared to ND at 26 percent or the U.S. at 28 percent. Sixty-five percent of the Spirit Lake population between 20 and 64 years of age are in the labor force (labor force includes unemployed who were actively searching for employment); 55 percent of the labor force population is employed, lower than the state (85 percent) and national levels (78 percent). The median household income on Spirit Lake reservation in 2006–2010 was $26,118, much lower than the state ($46,781) and national ($51,914) levels. Nearly half (47.8 percent) of the reservation's residents live below the poverty level, much higher than state ((12.3 percent) and national (13.8 percent) levels.

The U.S. Census Bureau reports that 57 percent of Spirit Lake children live in poverty as compared to ND's rate of 14 percent. The local school systems all have higher rates (78 percent) of students (mostly Native children) who qualify for reduced and free lunches than the state rate (25 percent).

The CCA provides much detail and information on the health, education, economic, and housing status and needs of the Spirit Lake community, as well as a summary on life satisfaction and the most important needs (priorities) for the Spirit

Lake Tribe. There were 18 items rated as 'very important' for the needs section of the CCA and at the top of the list is child safety/protection, followed by housing and employment, then health/behavioral health items. It is important to note that all 18 items were rated above a four with five = Very Important. Respondents noted that access to health care services, particularly mental health/social services/substance abuse treatment, along with better quality of services, are important factors influencing outcomes. To improve child safety/protection, respondents want more community, child and youth activities on the reservation that are planned and coordinated, especially to address youth risk factors for drug/alcohol use. The CCA developed a chart of recommendations, which is organized by needs as identified by the respondents, and includes other studies/reports. The recommendations provide a framework for addressing child safety/protection for the Spirit Lake community.

Health and education go hand in hand. Education is the pathway to address the various issues affecting the protection and safety of children but to pursue education, there must be some semblance of health and well-being. Native people have been taught dependency and various federal policies have had a detrimental impact that contributes to the dependency lifestyle. Poverty and hopelessness limit aspirations and it is a debilitating cycle that is compounded by alcohol and drug abuse. Reinforcement of Dakota life values is core to the work at CCCC and for all tribal colleges. Revitalizing cultural knowledge and Dakota values that are rooted in language is the mission of CCCC. Tribal college research is documenting that Native college students who have a strong cultural identity, are having successful college outcomes.

I strongly believe that there is an abundance of data and reports regarding the social, education, and economic disparities, as well as on child abuse, neglect, death, or suicides on American Indians that informs the implementation of the *Native American Children's Safety Act of 2016*. We need coordinated resource development for tribal-specific response, such as the Spirit Lake Comprehensive Community Assessment. Resources, including support, for training and education of tribal members to become the professionals needed for social services, addiction counseling, culturally based family services, lawyers, doctors, teachers, child care providers, and so on, must be a priority goal. Resources for family homes and facilities to provide the services, and built for North Dakota weather and geography, must be a priority goal. Stronger networking of federal agencies, state programs, tribal programs, and private organizations must be encouraged so services are integrated and available where the people reside.

Families need help that is not punitive and that encourages and supports them in a good way, utilizing incremental steps. Head Start is a wonderful model that does what it can toward helping families and supporting the development of their children. CCCC has administered the Spirit Lake Head Start program since January 2014 and currently serves approximately 140 children, ages infant to 5 years old. CCCC Head Start has a prenatal component wherein, we track down the pregnant woman and help to get her into services. The baby is guaranteed a slot in the Head Start program with the mother's cooperation. As we counsel the pregnant women, there are a myriad of problems she is trying to address and generally, the mothers are very young and lack support or knowledge of what to do or how/who to reach out to. The CCCC Head Start prenatal nurse usually does this counseling in her car, as the young mother-to-be is staying somewhere that is not "her" home and she is afraid of consequences for talking to a nurse.

CCCC Head Start is a mandated reporter for suspected child abuse or neglect. Since January 2017, our program has filed sixteen, SFN 960s to the Bureau of Indian Affairs (BIA) Child Protection Services (CPS) in Fort Totten, ND that I am aware of—that is an average of one per week! Our issue is that the Head Start staff (usually a Family Services Advocate/FSA, but sometimes the nurses) do not hear back on the filed 960, so we do not know if it has been received, that a review/investigation will be conducted, and most importantly is the child or children safe and being cared for in a good way. In comparison, on occasion the Head Start staff file a 960 with Ramsey County and per the staff, ". . .within an hour of sending in the 960, the Ramsey County Child Protection Services (CPS) has called to verify receipt of the report, ask questions, and to acknowledge that they are following up." We only want assurances that the child or children are being protected and in a safe environment.

The CCCC Head Start program has made significant progress in the three years we have managed it, including securing funding to build a center that is centrally located on the reservation and desperately needed for the community. This is a collaboration between the Spirit Lake Tribe and the College, with CCCC securing two USDA Community Facilities loans for $7.6 million for the construction, plus $900,000 from the Office of Head Start. The Spirit Lake Tribe is making the payments for the loans which started in March 2017. The new Head Start Center is 42,000 square feet, brick, with 19 classrooms to serve 185 children. It will have a nurse's station, commercial kitchen, heated bus garage, office/reception area, and a multi-purpose room for parent/teacher training. The center is for the children and families of Spirit Lake and will open in the fall 2017. We are grateful for the USDA loans, but it is frustrating that loans had to be utilized, as the Spirit Lake Dakota reservation is a designated Promise and Strike Force Zone (extreme poverty, high unemployment, and limited economic development). I have requested consideration to have the loans waived, decreased, or minimized due to extreme economic hardship.

Another component for Indian Head Start programs is the need for credentialed teachers, social workers, nurses, and administrators who are tribal members. CCCC utilizes Department of Education, Title III grant program resources for professional development of faculty and staff, including Head Start employees, and we have six tribal members working on bachelor's degrees in Early Childhood Education (ECE) and another four in social work. To meet Head Start standards, we project a need for 25 teachers with bachelor's degrees in ECE for the new Head Start Center.

The tribal colleges and universities system (TCUs), via the American Indian Higher Education Consortium (AIHEC), has requested the restoration of the funding for the TCU/Head Start Partnership program, that helped TCUs build capacity in early childhood education by providing scholarships and stipends for Indian Head Start teachers and teacher assistants in TCU ECE programs. AIHEC has requested $8 million be designated for the TCU/Head Start Partnership program, as authorized in PL 110–134, so TCUs can provide high-quality, culturally-appropriate training for teachers and staff in the Indian Head Start programs.

Training and recruitment of individuals and families to become foster parents is another important priority for the Spirit Lake community, and an essential component toward the safety and protection of children. Multi-disciplinary teams led by social services, are necessary to nurture collaboration, wrap-around services, and to provide advocacy for healthy families. The training and development of tribal people is essential toward facilitating change and improving home and family life.

The United Nations articulates that education is a fundamental human right:

> Education is recognized as both a human right in itself and an indispensable means of realizing other human rights and fundamental freedoms, the primary vehicle by which economically and socially marginalized peoples can lift themselves out of poverty and obtain a means to participate fully in their communities. Education is increasingly recognized as one of the best long-term financial investments that States can make.

> (United Nations. (2009) State of the World's Indigenous Peoples. New York, NY: Author. Retrieved from *http://www.un.org/esa/socev/unpfii/documents/SOWIP/en/SOWIP_web.pdf*)

The protection of, and justice for, Indian children in the implementation of the *Native American Children's Safety Act of 2016* must be rooted in educational opportunities that are funded adequately. Those opportunities must be available at the local/tribal level and culturally relevant. Education for parents/families to understand the dynamics of life and doing a better job toward the development and well-being of their children. Education for the professional development of tribal members to staff social services, to be the teachers, nurses, or doctors. This is the work of Cankdeska Cikana Community College and all the TCUs.

We look forward to working together to protect and provide safe environments for all sacred little ones. . .wakanheza. Thank you (pidamaya) for the opportunity to provide testimony.

Mitakuye oyasin. . .all my relations (we are all related.)

Senator HOEVEN. Thank you, Dr. Lindquist. Thanks, again, also, for—not only the work you do here, but for hosting us today.

I do have questions for the panel. Before I do that, though, I do want to also acknowledge Judge Foughty, a State District Court Judge who is here.

Thank you for your work on behalf of Native American children, as well. I appreciate it so much.

Also, we have, from the ranking member staff of the Committee, Tom Udall of New Mexico: Several of his staff members were good enough to join us: Both Kim Moxley and Catelin Aiwohi. So I'd like to thank both of them for joining us, as well.

With that, I do want to turn to Secretary Black and ask you: As part of the background checks required under the Native American Children's Safety Act, fingerprint checks are being conducted.

And while they're needed to help ensure the safety of children in foster care placements, they still take time to run.

And so, without those checks in place, there's a period of time where children may be at risk. So can you talk a little bit about how you address that.

And also, what you're doing to make sure that that fingerprint check, background check, is done as expeditiously as possible. And of course, under the law now, it has to be done on any of the adults in a foster home.

And again, it's important to point out that's not something that just affects Spirit Lake; that affects every Reservation in the country. So if you could, go through that and let me know how you're handling it.

Mr. BLACK. Sure. Well, we recognize that there are time lapses in getting back full background checks done, you know, based on a varied number of reasons.

But one of the ways that we've been able to address it here at Spirit Lake is we have provided the Social Services Program with portable fingerprint machines.

So that enables them to go into the homes for emergency placement, relative placement, and get those fingerprint checks and get them back.

Then, we FedEx them. We have hired a third-party contractor to conduct those activities for us, so it enables us to FedEx those fingerprints to them.

And we have been getting those back in anywhere from three to five days, which has really helped us to speed up that process and limit the amount of time that a child may be in a home that doesn't have a complete background check.

Senator HOEVEN. What about, under the legislation, the Secretary of Interior is required to issue guidance, following Tribal consultation, on follow-up background checks.

So obviously, these are for foster homes across the country where children have been placed in foster homes, and background checks had not been done because they weren't required to under the law, prior to this legislation.

So obviously, after consultation, the Secretary of the Interior is required to put that into place. I think that the guidance is due by June 3rd of 2018.

So how is that process coming, and what's your estimated timeline on getting that done?

Mr. BLACK. Sure. Well, we are currently on-schedule to get that done by the deadline, June 2018.

We have the guidance issued where, as I said in my testimony, we're planning on conducting Tribal consultations this coming fall.

Then, we would be able to take the information gathered from those and be able to develop the guidance by the deadline.

But in the meantime, we've currently got a team of folks that are working together and looking at social services agencies across the country, both Tribal and BIA, to look at best practices and look at those things that they are doing currently out there that may be something that we can apply across—you know, across Indian Country as best practices on how not only they're conducting their social services programs and Child Protection Services, but how they're doing the background checks.

Similar to the activities that we're doing here at Spirit Lake: Is that something we can replicate across the country and that Tribal Social Services programs can replicate, as well?

Senator HOEVEN. Right. That's exactly, I guess, the second part of my question, which you anticipated:

How are you coming in the meantime, making sure that you are doing checks while you're working on completing the guidelines.

Mr. BLACK. Yes, sir.

Senator HOEVEN. Okay. I turn to Administrator Hatch. The Administration for Children and Families conducted an on-site review of the Spirit Lake Social Services Program in 2014; published its findings and recommendations in June of 2014.

And these recommendations were, you know, intended to help improve the Tribal Social Services system.

Now, one of the notable items in the report was ACF's offer for no-cost Title IV–E training to Spirit Lake Tribal Social Services, BIA, and members of the Tribal staff.

So—and this touches, I think, on some of the comments that both the Chairwoman and President Lindquist made in terms of training and resources.

And so, I'd like you to address that in terms of training; other assistance, both technical assistance and funding assistance; and then, also, what else can you do?

How can you help get the issue of not only training but resources, which both Dr. Lindquist and Chairwoman Pearson talked about?

What else can we do to get that training; get that technical assistance; and, hopefully, get some more resources?

Ms. HATCH. Thank you very much, Mr. Chairman, for the question. As you stated, in 2014, the ACF provided seven recommendations primarily to the Tribe on areas for improving practices and systems across the entire child welfare system here on the Reservation.

And the ACF has continued to partner with the Tribe closely with ongoing dialogue and technical assistance related to the implementation of those. More broadly, there are a handful of things I would like to mention.

First is, as I've said, we have developed an ongoing partnership with the Tribe through regional program management within my regional office, being available for regular phone consultation and site visits on a number of questions.

That is an ongoing engagement that's a priority to us at the Administration for Children and Families.

We're also active participants in the social services coalition here that provides—that brings together a number of interested parties focused on a wide array of improvement areas related to social services here on the Spirit Lake Nation.

Finally, there is within ACF what is called a Capacity Building Center for Tribes, the CBCT, in which, at the request of the Tribe, we can provide in-depth, ongoing technical assistance on particular issues.

In 2015, as part of the Capacity Building Center for Tribes, we worked closely in the development of what are called Child Welfare Practice Maps.

That practice map: essentially, takes all aspects of child welfare, from intake—from the time a call is received related to a concern about the welfare of a child—through the system.

That mapping exercise is essential to developing clarity of understanding; common understanding of roles; even a common, vernacular or language that interested stakeholders can have related to child welfare practice.

And we've done that in close partnership with the Tribe as well as with our partners in BIA, the Community College, Casey Family Programs, and so on.

And we stand by that technical advice and the CBCT at the request of the Tribe for ongoing technical assistance and training.

Senator HOEVEN. Dr. Lindquist talked about the Head Start program that the College is working on with the support of the Tribal Council.

Is there anything you can do to help there, in terms of helping them fund the Head Start and bringing resources, assistance, training?

You know, can you help with a specific project like that? Because it's not just about keeping children safe; it's about helping them thrive, and getting them educated, and helping them succeed.

Ms. HATCH. Thank you, Chairman. Absolutely, we can work closely on that project. Head Start is within the Administration for Children and Families, as you know.

And I'll follow up immediately with staff in my office about opportunities to partner closely with——

Senator HOEVEN. So that's the kind of thing—we're going to have these hearings across the country on various issues.

Today, it's on, you know, child safety. That's not only an issue on-reservation; that's an issue off-reservation.

But the point I'm trying to make is: These are bigger issues that go across the Reservation; that go across our society.

So for example, when we go out and we talk to people who are working at the local level to make a positive difference, which these people are: Which Chairwoman Pearson and Dr. Lindquist are.

I mean, they're doing this every day. So when they bring up something like what I think sounds like just a marvelous project, the Head Start project, if we can actually work on some of the specifics that they bring up to us, I think those are the examples that not only would make a meaningful difference here and create a positive reaction, but the kind of things that other places could emulate.

Because then, somewhere, someone else somewhere else on another reservation in this state or some other state will go, "Oh, look what they did with that Head Start program. And gee, maybe we could do something like that, too."

So your last comments I think are very positive, much appreciated, and exactly what we're looking for.

I hope good things come out of this discussion today and the other discussions that we'll be having, both in D.C. and across the country.

But think about it: Even just that, just that one step, how meaningful that could be if you help them accomplish this project.

So I would really appreciate it, and we'll certainly take you up on your offer to follow up with both of them on that project.

And I think, if you find a way to help them, that would be really wonderful and a great example of what we're hoping to accomplish with these hearings as we do them.

With that, then I would turn to Chairwoman Pearson. And Administrator Hatch, kind of, led into exactly what I was hoping to create:

To find some opportunities to bring some assistance and to do some things that could be meaningful on your end and other places.

But you started your testimony and mentioned some of the regulations and some of the difficulties that you have in regard to working with BIA in terms of Child Protection Services, and so forth.

So since we have Secretary Black here, what are some specific things you think he could do that would really help make a difference in that regard: That would help the Tribal Council in terms of taking care of kids?

Ms. PEARSON. By assuring us that, you know, our children are being taken care of, but also working openly with us.

I've sat in several meetings with, you know, the BIA and the Tribal Social Services Departments, and it was always a finger-pointing session.

So I feel that, you know, if we can openly work with each other and, kind of, put our issues aside and think of who we're there to work for.

We're there to look and watch out and protect the children of our Nation. But instead of that, we argue over whose job it is to do these things.

We need to work together. And I do believe that, you know, Mr. Black: If he can hold his staff responsible, I think that's going to, you know, kind of alleviate some of the issues that we've been going through.

Another thing that I look at in protecting children: I like the fact that, you know, we're in jobs that we're mandated to report these things.

I've always had to report them due to my own position because I'm there to protect these children, whether they vote or not. They're little children.

And, you know, I sit in a position where I can speak for them. And I will speak up for them because they're not going to be able to do it.

No one else is going to do it, so I will do it. And I will assure— as long as I'm here, I'm going to assure that these children are protected and they have, you know, what everybody should be looking out for.

Another thing that I think we need to do is we need to start holding their parents responsible.

We need to take some of these—you know, some of the stress off ourselves but put it back on those parents because we do have programs that will help them.

And if we can get more resources, I think, you know, we can turn this thing around, you know, a whole lot more than we have here.

I come in here in 2014; I haven't seen it move that far along. But, you know, I want to see some type of action now.

And I appreciate the fact that you came—you know, you've come here, because in 2012, '13, I believe, we had a hearing such as this, and no one came out after that.

I understand, you know, the case loads you carry, as well. But, you know, our children are just as important.

And I've always said that, and I'm going to do what I can for them. I have a passion there for them, and you know, I just want to make sure that they're well cared for.

I had that kind of a childhood, and I expect everyone else to be able to provide that same thing for their grandchildren.

I may not have been rich, but you know, I was able to live in a home that I felt secure; I felt loved. I was never hungry, and I was not cold.

And, you know, it might seem a little outdated and everything, but I think that's what we need today. We need to go back a little bit and pick up some pieces and move forward with it.

Sure, we need resources. But, you know, we also need that compassion within our families; within our community.

And I need any help I can get here at Spirit Lake, you know, I would really appreciate it.

And I've worked with Mr. Black before. Ms. Hatch, you know, I look forward to working with you, as well. And also you, Senator Hoeven. Thank you.

Senator HOEVEN. Yes. You know, you've been Chairwoman I don't know how many terms. But I know we worked together when I was governor, and that was a while ago.

Ms. PEARSON. Yes.

Senator HOEVEN. So I know you care; I know what your commitment is. And Dr. Lindquist talked about filing the 690s with the BIA, you know, and expressed concern about hearing back.

And then, talked about, when they're filed with Benson County, they hear back right away.

And so, I would ask Secretary Black to talk about that, both in terms of how you can be—how can BIA respond to the concerns that the Chairwoman brought up, that Dr. Lindquist brought up, both in terms of being responsive now and also working with the county and state on children's social services because you can leverage your efforts that way, as well.

So what can we do to make sure the BIA is more responsive? Is it an ombudsman? I mean, what do we do to, kind of, make sure that that—close that gap? Address that concern.

Mr. BLACK. Well, sure. Let me just address a little bit: First of all, I can definitely say I can commit my staff to working with the Tribe.

All the issues that the Chairwoman worked out: I don't think that's anything that's out of hand.

I liked hearing the statement that, you know, we can't be pointing fingers, either us back at the Tribe or the Tribe back at us.

It's a matter of really sitting down and seeing where we are and where we want to go with the program. So I think that's something we can definitely commit to doing.

The 960 reports: I don't know exactly the process and why people aren't getting back. I do know, you know, that last year alone, we had over 560, I believe it was, 960s filed here at Fort Totten.

We have a staff of about three to four social workers working all of those 960s. So we've got about—at any one time, probably about a 30-to-1 ratio of cases per social worker.

So, I mean, there are some resource issues that we have to work out. But, at the same time, if there's a way that we can work to ensure that we get some kind of a response back.

I know, when we took over the program in 2012, you know, there was a lot of issues with the 960s: How they were being processed or not being processed.

We've gone through some efforts, some lengthy efforts, to make sure that we're able to address those more expeditiously and make sure that we are, you know, running through the intake process on all of those 960s.

And then, we've also—you know, I had mentioned previously— or, I didn't mention here, but I had previously testified in different hearings about some of the other efforts that we had going on here, you know.

And one of those key efforts is the—I think it's called the "multidisciplinary team," where it's, basically, a coalition of all of the service providers in this area, including the state; the county; the Tribe; the BIA; the College.

And they had been meeting regularly—at least about once a month—to really sit down and identify all of the different issues: What resources these different parties could bring to the table.

And those are the things that we need to keep going in an effort to really make this program what everybody wants it to be.

Senator HOEVEN. So what I would ask you before you leave is: Ask—or, get from the Chairwoman her top three priorities.

And then, what I would like from you is a response back as to how you plan to address them, and who is going to be the pointperson to work with the Chairwoman to do that. Would that be all right?

Mr. BLACK. I'll do that.

Senator HOEVEN. Okay.

Mr. BLACK. Pointperson's sitting right behind me, so——

Senator HOEVEN. Okay, that would be good. And then, to Dr. Lindquist: Your college serves as the lead institution administering the Tribal Health Profession Opportunity Grant Program.

So I want you to tell me about it: Where it's working; where it's not; how we help make sure that, you know, it is of some assistance to you and to others that are trying to use it across the country.

Dr. LINDQUIST. So HPOG, Health Profession Opportunity Grant from the Department of Health and Human Services, Administration for Children and Families:

Cankdeska Cikana Community College is in the second year of a second award for this program. And our program is called Next Steps.

Senator HOEVEN. Called———

Dr. LINDQUIST. Next Steps.

Senator HOEVEN. Next Steps, okay.

Dr. LINDQUIST. And it's actually—our director for Next Steps is Skip Longie, or Phillip "Skip" Longie, former chairperson of the Spirit Lake Dakota Nation, so I'm sure you're familiar with Skip.

Senator HOEVEN. Yes.

Dr. LINDQUIST. And unfortunately, he was on travel this week at a regional meeting in Denver regarding the Next Steps program and HPOG.

We are in our second year of funding for the second phase of this. It is a statewide program to provide support services to low-income students who are enrolled in health-related professions or programs of study.

This includes from CNA, certified nurse assistant; certified medical assistant; LPN; RN; BSN; social work; nutrition; and actually, we have a paramedic student right now.

The program is located across North Dakota, so we have mentor staff in Fargo; in Bismarck; in Minot; and Fort Totten.

And we collaborate and partner with United Tribes Technical College; Sitting Bull College; Lake Regions State College; UND; NDSU; North Dakota State School of Science; Williston State College; Dickinson College; Bottineau; and Minot State University.

So it's a collaboration among institutions led by Cankdeska Cikana Community College, specific to supporting students in those disciplines.

We currently have 70 students in the program; 39 are Native students. They are on-track at different levels to graduate in these disciplines.

I believe the key to success for this program is the mentoring. It's one-on-one mentoring.

And so, we have mentors on-staff who are professionals, either nurses or nutritionist; et cetera; social worker, and that. But they keep in constant contact with these students to keep them on-track.

The other thing that is most important about Next Steps and this Health Professions Opportunity Grant is that support services includes not just tuition and fees.

And we don't—at the bigger institutions, we don't pay all of the tuition; we pay a portion of it.

But we do pay for books; we pay for licensure; we pay for child care; transportation; uniforms.

So it's, like, an all-encompassing type of a program specific to what these students need to be a good college student and to complete and succeed in these programs.

It's a very important program; it's very successful. I wasn't able to get the data from our first phase of the program on how many people we have placed.

But I know it's close to 100 people in North Dakota and across the state, beginning with quality service providers: So the home-based care technicians and professionals, and that.

Senator HOEVEN. So these are 100 people you've placed in——

Dr. LINDQUIST. Across North Dakota. It's like, four summers ago, we trained 18 CNAs in Fargo/Moorhead.

Most of those—I think all of them are Native people in Fargo/Moorhead, and they were all placed in the in-patient care system in the Fargo/Moorhead area as CNAs.

Senator HOEVEN. And does the funding pay for all of their education?

Dr. LINDQUIST. Yes.

Senator HOEVEN. Part of it?

Dr. LINDQUIST. It pays for the majority of it. Now, at the bigger institutions where there's higher tuitions, we only pay a portion. We limit it. But at the smaller institutions, we're a little bit more affordable.

And part of not paying 100 percent of the tuition is to, again, make sure we promote a sense of personal responsibility in helping our students to understand budgeting, budget management, in that, "Oh, this is really a benefit."

And we want them to participate in that obligation.

Senator HOEVEN. How many years have you administered the HPOG program?

Dr. LINDQUIST. Pardon?

Senator HOEVEN. How many years have you administered the program?

Dr. LINDQUIST. This—total, this would be our seventh year.

Senator HOEVEN. Seventh? Okay.

Dr. LINDQUIST. Yes.

Senator HOEVEN. And then, has the funding been steady? down? up? What's the funding status?

Dr. LINDQUIST. Flatline.

Senator HOEVEN. Flatline?

Dr. LINDQUIST. Pretty much flatline.

Senator HOEVEN. So it's been the same?

Dr. LINDQUIST. In the scope of it, the first five years was Native students only. And now, this second go-around—again, we're in the second year of the second phase of funding—it's opened up to low-income students across the State of North Dakota.

Senator HOEVEN. And is there a prescribed number of years for which you administer the funds, or is that ongoing until change?

Dr. LINDQUIST. It's a five-year funded grant.

Senator HOEVEN. So five years at a time?

Dr. LINDQUIST. Right.

Senator HOEVEN. And do you—off the top of your head, do you recall the amount that you get each year?

Dr. LINDQUIST. I'm sure I'm going to be incorrect, but I think it's between $1.5 to $2 million, roughly——

Senator HOEVEN. Okay.

Dr. LINDQUIST. —but I might be off. I can check it, but——

Senator HOEVEN. And is there a formula it follows?

Dr. LINDQUIST. I believe there is a formula when the grant is announced as to if you're selected and the amount that you're going to receive.

Senator HOEVEN. So you're in year two of the second five?

Dr. LINDQUIST. Right, right.

Senator HOEVEN. Okay.

Dr. LINDQUIST. It is a great example, again, of collaboration between Federal Government, federal agency; a local Tribal community college; and then, networking, which we're——

I think Native people, Native communities are really good at doing that because it's somewhat cultural.

We like to get along; we like relationships. And, you know, in North Dakota, we know everybody. We know each other.

And so, there's some great partnerships among the institutions, but also, I think, among the providers.

So Altru System in Grand Forks, Sanford in Bismarck and Fargo: We have great partnerships, and we facilitate that.

Lake Region State College, the Dakota nursing program, is a great partner and has helped us to open doors and to expand what we do.

Senator HOEVEN. You offer a degree here in social work. Are you able to retain many of those people that you graduated with a social work degree; and then, are you able to recruit people into the program?

Right? Because that makes such a difference in terms of getting at what we're talking about, which is taking care of kids.

So tell me a little bit about, you know, kind of, how many you're able to train with a degree in social work.

Do they go on, then? Do they get a baccalaureate here? Do they go on to somewhere else?

You know, how many are you able to recruit back or keep here, and are you able to attract people into the program? I mean, could you train more than you're training now?

Dr. LINDQUIST. Mr. Chairman and Senator Hoeven, this is a brand-new program that we just implemented in 2015.

This is a partnership between Cankdeska Cikana Community College, the University of North Dakota social work department, and Sitting Bull College.

Now, my college, our college here in Fort Totten, Spirit Lake, is an associate degree-granting institution.

And so, we really like these partnerships: The two-plus-two. So we do the first two years: The gen eds, the basic studies. Yes, we know that they want to go to nursing or to social work and that, so we're just beginning.

We have eight students, approximately, if I remember my numbers right—and I just looked at the numbers this morning, but I'm having a senior moment.

We have eight students in the program right now at the junior level. So they're at UND, but they're here. They're UND students, and that.

If we could have something like Next Steps for social work— which we do, because social work is included in Next Steps, we only have a couple of those 70 students on the social work track.

We're projecting, when we open up our Head Start center—and as I've worked with the Tribe for Tribal Social Services, I have personally estimated that this community needs 15 social workers.

For our Head Start program alone, we have four family services advocates, FSAs, who, I think, out of the four we have on-staff right now, only one has a bachelor's degree, and it's a BSW.

And the goal is for the all three of them—and the other three are, you know, slowly.

The model is there now, and this partnership is going to be able to facilitate our students staying home—even though we do want them to get off the Reservation to have a better world experience, either at UND or at Sitting Bull College, in the social worker system someplace—Casey Family Foundation in Seattle or Denver, and that.

But knowing that they can be home-based, and that those support services are there toward their success.

So I'm very optimistic. So I think our first class will be in maybe a year, but probably two years out, where we're going to have four to five completing the bachelors in social work degree.

Senator HOEVEN. Right. So this is—I mean, this is a very good program. This is a very good partnership, once again.

It seems to me that you're creating the leveraging of resources we need to try to get more resources on the target.

You are talking about a program where not only you and Sitting Bull College are involved, but also the University of North Dakota, which has very strong Native American education programs, so that's further leverage; including state and federal funds; and then, tying it in with the Tribal Council and other support through the Head Start.

Seems to me this is the kind of initiative where you're really bringing a lot of groups together to accomplish something.

So again, you know, anything we can do to help support that Head Start effort. And that's why I'm so pleased that Administrator Hatch is willing to help there.

And then, I'm going to turn back to you, Administrator. And this one goes to Secretary Black, as well.

And I think this is probably a challenge everywhere, but how do we get more foster homes? How do we establish more safe homes, whether it's on the Reservation here or anywhere else?

You know, what can we do collaboratively to get more foster homes available so that we're ready to go when we need that help?

Ms. HATCH. Thank you very much for that question, Chairman Hoeven. And you're exactly right that the attraction and recruitment, training and support of high-quality foster families is an issue far beyond any particular Reservation, it's a nationwide issue.

One of the areas of support that is available through our Capacity Building Centers is related to foster parent recruitment.

And I believe that, through the Capacity Building Center for Tribes, at least one Tribe or Tribal consortium has made that an area of focus, and I'd be happy to follow up to provide that kind of——

Senator HOEVEN. Well, yes.

Particularly if they've had success, it would be good to know what that is and then try to get that out to the other reservations.

Ms. HATCH. That's exactly right. And that's one of the things that these Centers emphasize, is peer-sharing. So where there's a success; where there's a lesson learned——

Senator HOEVEN. Right.

Ms. HATCH. —making sure that others can benefit from that learning. The targets with foster care recruitment are about increasing the number of foster families; the training, the quality, the suitability of them; and reducing the administrative burden so that, as Chairwoman Pearson mentioned, the uptake time can be reduced from a year down to a minimum amount of time so that it can be an efficient and effective process.

Senator HOEVEN. Chairwoman Pearson, if you would, talk a little bit about the Tiwahe Initiative.

Actually, I think you were one of the first four pilot programs for Tiwahe, and I just wonder what your thoughts are in terms of the program.

Ms. PEARSON. I think it's really beneficial for the Tribe. In fact, today, I believe our Tiwahe staff and some of our employees that attended the Tiwahe Conference down in Arizona are traveling back.

So unfortunately, they couldn't be here today to, you know, answer any questions or give us anything.

But the Tiwahe program has been doing real good. They've been working with families; they've been working with children.

There's several things that they've been doing such as, you know, assisting with the social service office, as well.

They're located across from each other: You know, west of Fort Totten, here. They have, I believe, a staff of three.

And you had mentioned earlier Ms. Hatch about the mapping project there, and that's what they've taken on themselves.

So I'm looking to, you know, see that completed and what—you know, how we can work to make our jobs, I guess, a little easier, and take on some of the job duties that it includes.

The Tiwahe, along with the Casey Foundation, have been really helpful here on the Reservation.

We've gone to a lot of meetings with them; we've gone to a lot of trainings with them. And, you know, I think, by working collaboratively like that, you know, we can—and I enjoy it because more people know about the children.

I mean, everybody is aware. There's more people aware of what some of the children are going through.

So that, kind of, hold us all responsible to make sure that that child is kept safe.

And, you know, by doing that, I also want to mention a little bit about the little Welfare Committee that we put together.

They also go through and assure that our foster care licenses are all—you know, there's a checklist that goes with that.

They go through it; they make sure that everything is attached before any of the licenses are signed.

Myself, along with the BIA superintendent, are the ones that sign the licenses out here.

And when those aren't complete, then we don't sign. So it's just assuring that these children are kept safe.

And, you know, by using all these other resources from everyone, Tiwahe, kind of, came in at a—you know, I wasn't too familiar with them.

But now I am, and I see where they're doing a lot to benefit, like I said, our families and our children.

I'd like to keep them around forever, but I don't know how their funding is going to last or, you know, how long it's going to last, or they might pull it or something. But nevertheless, they've helped us a lot here.

Senator HOEVEN. Okay.

Ms. PEARSON. The Casey Foundation has also been another, you know, big help to us out here.

And I give that credit to Former Chairman McDonald. You know, he brought it in. And in fact, the day that I came in, the Casey Foundation people were here, too.

So when we made our transition, that's—he was going out, and I was coming in, but we were all working together, you know, and that's what it was on: The Casey Foundation and these other programs that came in to help.

And I think we all, kind of, came in at a time when things were a lot worse than they are today. But they're improving, but not fast enough, I guess.

Senator HOEVEN. Chairwoman, you've always been a stabilizing force, a steadying force on the Reservation, and it's much appreciated.

I guess the last question I have for each of you would be: The BIA is getting guidance on implementation of the legislation to make sure that background checks are done in foster homes and that the foster homes are safe.

So just any thoughts that each of you would have just as we wrap up, here, in terms of what you want to make sure that the BIA is looking at as they undertake that effort?

So I guess I'll start with Administrator Hatch; and go to the Chairwoman and Dr. Lindquist; and then, just come back to you, Mike, for—to respond.

Ms. HATCH. Thank you. ACF works very closely with the BIA and has been and will continue to work very closely to ensure that the rollout of the criminal background check requirement is done as smoothly and as easily as possible, and is aligned with what we already understand in child welfare practice, and is implemented related to the title IV–E background check requirements so we have ongoing conversations and will continue to do so to make sure that we have the best learning and sharing of best practices as possible.

Senator HOEVEN. Okay. Chairwoman?

Ms. PEARSON. What I'd like to get your support on is to see if we can license more off-reservation homes, or if we can go in that direction, because we definitely don't have enough here on the Reservation.

And if the same rules can apply there because, as you heard earlier, Ramsey County would—you know, their response time back to us was, you know, like, in a few hours.

So if we could apply those same rules and stuff to homes off the Reservation, and if we can license homes off the Reservation, because, like I said, we don't have enough homes here on the Reservation for our need.

That's, I believe, all. But I'd like you to consider that. Also, before—I'm going to bring Tiwahe back up. But, you know, I'd ask that you support that and——

Senator HOEVEN. Right.

Ms. PEARSON. —make sure they hang around for a good long time.

Senator HOEVEN. Well, that's why I asked about it: To put it in the record that you think it's helpful. That's helpful, in terms of getting funding.

Ms. PEARSON. Okay, thank you.

Senator HOEVEN. Dr. Lindquist?

Dr. LINDQUIST. My question or comment, I guess: How do we help you to have professional Native staff that will stay here for the long haul?

I have met a few of the social workers that have come from wherever they've come from because sometimes they'll come here and have lunch in our cafeteria or cafe.

Good people, good-hearted people, and qualified people who really mean well. But they've only been assigned for three months or four months or six months, and it's too inconsistent.

And so, how do we get a core group of professional social workers—the gamut: Paralegal, forensic—to do these multi-disciplinary tasks?

And so, as the president of the Tribal College, I'm trying to help by supporting my students, but it's going to take a little bit of time.

But there has to be more we can do together. And not just the BIA, but other agencies: The Indian Health Service, you know, and that.

How do we work on this better together to have that core group of people here for the long haul?

Senator HOEVEN. Michael, I'll let you wrap up.

Mr. BLACK. All right. I'll get it wrapped up, hot dog. You know, basically—you know, thank you for the comments.

And I'm going to touch on Dr. Lindquist's comment here first real quick: And I do look forward to working with you and anybody else that would like to work with us on recruitment and retention.

We have had a—you know, just an extremely difficult time in recruiting staff, you know, particularly up here during a lot of the issues that were going on.

But I think we're beyond those now, you know, to a certain point to where, hopefully, we are in a better place that we're able to recruit and retain people here at Spirit Lake.

But it's not just Spirit Lake where we have that issue, you know. Recruitment across the board for social workers right now has been extremely difficult.

And so, it is something that I think is going to take a larger group than just the two of us—maybe pulling a lot of other people to look at different ways: What kind of incentives and ideas can we come up with that will incentivize or, you know, help to recruit people and entice them to come to the Reservations and to work with our Indian children. So I'll look forward to being able to do that.

As far as the background checks and stuff go, you know, we look forward to, you know, looking at different ways that we can improve that process, you know, and not make it as onerous as it sometimes can be and make it as expeditious as it can be.

So we look forward to that, as well. But thank you for holding this today, sir. We appreciate it.

Senator HOEVEN. Secretary Black, thank you. You've been responsive to me when I've contacted you.

Before I was in this role as chairman, you've been responsive to me, and I appreciate that.

And so, whatever you can do to get the people working throughout the BIA to have your sense of responsiveness. I think if they had your sense of responsiveness, that that would help.

And so, let's start with a little effort along that line because the Chairwoman has asked for you to be responsive on a number of these things. Let's see how this goes.

But I think you have that—you really have always been that way with me, and I want to commend you on it: You, personally.

And then, with your leadership there—to try to create that sense of responsiveness throughout the BIA.

Again, I think they could learn it from you directly. So I don't know if that means that you need to get out in the field and just talk to people about how you do it—but I think, if they emulate you, that will help. I mean it very sincerely.

Mr. BLACK. Thank you. I appreciate that.

Senator HOEVEN. And, of course, that is an important part of leadership. Thank you for being here, and thank you for your testimony.

Thank you for your work on the Native American Children's Safety Act and, of course, many, many other issues.

Also, again, thank you, Administrator Hatch, for your willingness to follow up. For being here today; but then, your willingness to follow up on a specific like this very good Head Start initiative that Dr. Lindquist is working on with many others.

Chairwoman, we'll try to help on some of these issues. You've always, as I said earlier, both in my time as governor and my time as a senator, you have been a steady force for the Reservation. And that's a very important, very good thing.

And we'll continue to try to help, but we understand that there are a lot of challenges and that there aren't enough resources. We'll try to help with some of these areas.

And Dr. Lindquist: Again, thank you for hosting and for your leadership on these issues that—of course, your primary job is as an educator.

But these issues cut across so many aspects of important issues in terms of children's safety; quality of life; and really, as you said, starting to break some of the cycles of dependency and creating a better standard of living for everyone, not just for our—how did you term it? Our sacred young ones—but for all of us, right?

Dr. LINDQUIST. Wakanheza.

Senator HOEVEN. Yes, so thank you. I should have mentioned that Matthew Leiphon is here with Senator Heitkamp's staff, as well. So Matthew, thanks for joining us. We appreciate it very much.

And with that, we'll conclude the hearing. I should also mention that the record will be open for two weeks.

So if there is additional testimony that anyone wants to submit into the record, they can do so, and it will be part of the permanent record. Again, thank you so much. We're adjourned.

[Whereupon, at 3:15 p.m the oversight field hearing concluded.]

APPENDIX

STATEMENT OF HON. HEIDI HEITKAMP, U.S. SENATOR FROM NORTH DAKOTA

I'd like to thank Chairman Hoeven for holding this field hearing and for all of the witnesses and community members who are able to join today. This hearing is an opportunity for us to discuss the implementation of the Native American Children's Safety Act (NACSA)—a critically important step forward for improving the welfare of Native children in Spirit Lake, North Dakota, and Indian Country as a whole. I was proud to join Chairman Hoeven in advancing this legislation, and am thankful that Congress came together to pass it to enhance the protection of our Native youth.

The Spirit Lake reservation in particular has faced many challenges with its child welfare programs and there have been instances of severe child abuse and neglect. No child, regardless of their background, should ever have to endure abuse at the hands of those who are meant to provide safe and loving homes. It is the job of each and every one of us to ensure the protection of all children.

However, when tribal communities are challenged by inadequate resources and inaction by authorities to act in a child's best interest, protecting our most vulnerable becomes an uphill battle. It was the tragic state of child welfare on Spirit Lake that brought attention to how complex jurisdictional systems were failing tribal communities and the critical importance of conducting background checks when placing Native American children in foster-care homes. Now, we need to ensure the law is faithfully implemented so no child in need falls through the cracks.

We know that Native communities in isolated rural or remote areas are among the most underserved. How can we ensure that these communities are equipped with qualified professionals and adequate resources while often coping with a lack of suitable foster homes? How can we ensure that children are not being left in dangerous living situations while agencies are conducting background checks—a process that can take several weeks? These are the questions I hope we can answer. It's encouraging that the Bureau of Indian Affairs (BIA) is currently in the process of developing guidance under NACSA by identifying best practices in social services and exploring opportunities for increased coordination between tribal, state, and federal authorities. I also applaud the initiatives that Cankdeska Cikana Community College has taken to increase the number of social workers in Indian Country, and the progress the Spirit Lake Tribe and the BIA have made in improving operations at the Fort Totten Agency.

Native children suffer the second-highest rate of abuse or neglect of any ethnic group, with a maltreatment rate of about 50 percent higher than for white or Hispanic children. In North Dakota, Native children constitute nearly 30 percent of the state's child abuse victims. When children are exposed to such traumatic experiences, studies show it can have serious long-term impacts on health and neurological and behavioral development. Since my first year in office, I have been committed to addressing the causes and impact of childhood trauma, and ensuring these children are supported with proper care. Last year, my bill to create a Commission on Native Children was signed into law. The Commission will study the complex issues Native children face and make recommendations to make sure children living in Indian Country get the protections, as well as economic and educational tools to thrive. I am pleased that Russ McDonald, president of United Tribes Technical College, has been appointed to serve on this commission. He brings a wealth of knowledge and experience to the table which will be vital when the commission begins its work. And more recently, I reintroduced the Trauma-Informed Care for Children and Families Act (S. 774) to comprehensively tackle the long-term impacts of trauma among Native children and families.

We have a basic duty to ensure the protection of our children. This field hearing is an important step forward in fulfilling our commitments to Indian Country, and I hope we can gain some valuable insight on the best way to move forward on tho protection of our Native youth, who are the future of tribal communities. I look forward to continuing to work together with tribal leaders and my colleagues in the Senate to address the needs of Indian Country.

———

PREPARED STATEMENT OF THE NATIONAL INDIAN CHILD WELFARE ASSOCIATION, NATIONAL CONGRESS OF AMERICAN INDIANS, NATIONAL INDIAN EDUCATION ASSOCIATION, AND NATIONAL INDIAN HEALTH BOARD (FOUNDING PARTNERS OF THE FIRST KIDS 1ST INITIATIVE)

Introduction

The safety and well-being of a community's children is one of the highest responsibilities for any government. Tribal governments, like states, have a special obligation to ensure that their community's children are safe from harm like child abuse and neglect. The tools for helping meet this responsibility include establishment of clear policies, adequately resourced child protection infrastructure and services, well-trained workforce, well-coordinated and effective partnerships with federal and state partners, and easy and reliable access to national criminal databases and child abuse registries. We applaud the Chairman and Vice-Chairman for holding this oversight hearing and providing our organizations with an opportunity to share our experiences, thoughts, and recommendations regarding the implementation of the Native American Children's Safety Act and overall efforts to support the safety and well-being of Native children. Our testimony will focus on key challenges to successfully implementing the Native Children's Safety Act, barriers to creating effective child protection programming in Indian Country, and recommendations for addressing these challenges.

About First Kids 1st: The First Kids 1st Initiative is a national collaborative effort comprised of leading Native American organizations, allies, and partners from all backgrounds, focused on changing national, tribal, and state policy to create conditions in which American Indian and Alaska Native children can thrive. We are working to cultivate and nurture strategies and policies that build and strengthen equitable and local supports for vulnerable Native children in their communities. The Founding Partners formally joined together to support the healthy development of Native youth by coordinating efforts to transform the systems that have the greatest impact on Native youth and families-systems of health, child welfare, education, and governance. Learn more at: *www.FirstKids1st.org*

A Brief History of Criminal Background Checks for Tribally Licensed Foster Homes and Implications for Implementation of the Native American Children's Safety Act

Indian Child Protection and Family Violence Prevention Act (1988–1997). Following widespread reports that Native children were being physically and sexually abused in Bureau of Indian Affairs (BIA) run boarding schools in the 1980's Chairman McCain and Vice-Chairman Inouye of the Senate Committee on Indian Affairs held several hearings to further investigate and document the problem and solicit suggestions on how to prevent further exploitation of Native children. What followed was legislation that was enacted into law in 1990 entitled the Indian Child Protection and Family Violence Prevention Act (P.L. 101–630). The law mandated greater coordination between law enforcement and child protection agencies serving Native children on tribal lands, improved reporting standards before and during investigations of alleged child abuse and neglect involving Native children on tribal lands, required criminal background checks for the Bureau of Indian Affairs (BIA), Indian Health Services (IHS), and tribal employees with contact or control over Native children, and grant programs to address child abuse and domestic violence prevention and treatment for victims, including the establishment of regional child abuse resource centers for Indian Country. The grant programs were, and still are today, the only tribal specific prevention and treatment program funds for Native children who are at risk of being abused or have been abused.

The criminal background check requirements under the law were later interpreted by the BIA to also apply to licensing of tribal foster care homes. At the time, criminal background checks were primarily done by name (now referred to as Code X criminal background checks) and fingerprint cards. Electronic submission of digitized fingerprint scans became more common after 1997 when the Adoption and Safe Families Act (P.L. 105–89) established first ever federal requirements for criminal background checks for prospective foster families licensed by state agencies. Later in 2006 the Adam Walsh Child Protection and Safety Act added additional requirements for states and tribes regarding criminal background checks and checking of child abuse registries for prospective foster families. Training for tribes on how to conduct the criminal background checks required under the Indian Child

Protection and Family Violence Prevention Act was slow in coming and did not adequately address issues of differences in tribal infrastructure and resources for mandated activities, opportunity to work with state partners, and access to national criminal databases like those that the Federal Bureau of Investigation (FBI) operate. A few years after the law went into effect the BIA created a process for tribes to submit name-based criminal background checks, but the process was slow leading to delays of anywhere from one to six months in getting the check completed in some cases. Regulations and agency guidance was also slow to be developed and did not address key issues such as access to national criminal databases adding to an already challenging environment for implementation. The result was low awareness within Indian Country of the law's new requirements, widespread frustration at the difficulty in meeting the law's requirements with respect to criminal background checks, and a lack of uniformity in interpretation and implementation.

Tribes Working with States to Conduct Criminal Background Checks (1997–2013). Following the passage of the Adoption and Safe Families Act in 1997, increasing numbers of tribes began to look to their state partners to help them perform the background checks required under the Indian Child Protection and Family Violence Prevention Act, especially those tribes that had limited child welfare and law enforcement infrastructure. This tribal-state collaboration was also boosted by increasing numbers of tribes (over 120) that developed agreements with their states to operate the Title IV–E Foster Care and Adoption Assistance program, which contained the Adoption and Safe Families Act criminal background check requirements for states. While the state assistance was welcomed by tribes in over 14 states, there were some downsides to the partnership. Tribes found they had little control over what violations the state criminal background checks looked at and many states had gone far beyond the federal minimum requirements for these checks. In several states, tribes were only able to get a finding of pass or fail on the background checks that the state performed, which did little to empower tribes to work with prospective foster families to see if they would have passed a background check that was matched to the requirements of federal law or pursue expungement of a person's record when it seemed appropriate. Nonetheless, more and more tribes relied upon their states to provide this critical service in an effort to ensure safety of children placed in tribal foster care homes.

Changes in State's Ability to Assist Tribes (2014 to the present). In 2014, nearly 13 years after many states and tribes developed agreements on conducting criminal background checks for prospective foster families, Washington State and Oregon discovered that FBI Criminal Justice Information Services had concerns about whether these arrangements met federal mandates and security requirements for the sharing of criminal background information with tribes by states. Both Washington and Oregon felt they needed to cease offering tribes the option of doing criminal background checks for over a year while trying to sort out how to meet federal requirements. During this intervening process, it became obvious that the federal policy landscape for tribes to gain access to state criminal background check processes was more complicated than many had believed earlier. While the Indian Child Protection and Family Violence Prevention Act and Adam Walsh Child Protection and Safety Act specifically identified tribes as being authorized to receive criminal background check information from the FBI regarding foster home criminal background checks, other federal law required states to enact legislation listing who specifically was eligible to receive this information before the FBI would make criminal records available to state and local governments specifically (see Title II, Section 201 of Public Law 92–544, 86 Stat. from October 25, 1972). This enabling legislation exists in only a handful of states where tribes are licensing foster homes and relying on the state to assist them in their criminal background checks.

Federal Responses to Tribal Advocacy to Improve Access to National Crime Databases (2015 to the present). In 2015, after concerted efforts by tribes, NICWA, and NCAI to work with FBI Criminal Justice Information Services and BIA, two new opportunities to address criminal background checks barriers for tribes licensing foster homes were developed. The first was access to Code X name-based criminal background checks. These are typically used when placing a child in an emergency foster placement late at night or during the weekend when there is not time to do a more comprehensive criminal background check with fingerprints. The BIA provides this access through their Office of Justice Services. The second is the Tribal Access Program (TAP). The TAP program is a demonstration project sponsored by the Department of Justice to provide tribes with a more effective access to FBI national crime information systems for both civil and criminal purposes. In the TAP program the Department of Justice acts as the conduit for select tribes who have been approved to participate in the TAP program. Currently, 10 tribes have been selected to participate in the TAP program. The demonstration project is well suited for tribes that have resources to develop and maintain the necessary infrastructure to meet federal security requirements connected to the access of FBI operated national crime data information databases, but is not a good fit for smaller, less well resourced tribes that need a less costly and more administratively feasible option. While both of these programs are helpful and improve tribal access to national crime databases, they do not provide uniform and effective access for all tribes that are licensing foster families on tribal lands.

Overall, it is estimated that there are over 300 tribes that license or approve their own foster care homes on tribal lands. These homes are not only helpful to tribal children living on tribal lands, but also to states that often need to borrow these homes to place Native children that live off tribal lands to ensure that Native children remain connected to their extended families and tribal culture. Our analysis and experience tells us that with reduced access to states that are willing to do criminal background checks for tribes and are authorized under federal law to share this information, combined with limited capacity for many tribes to develop direct access to the FBI's national crime databases, implementation of the Native Children's Safety Act may suffer from some of the same ailments that has plagued implementation of the Indian Child Protection and Family Violence Prevention Act since its enactment in 1990.

Recommendations
    1) Harmonize current federal law requirements that impact tribal access to national crime databases so that all tribes that license their own foster care homes can have easy and effective access to submit, process, and receive criminal background check information related to the placement of Native children in tribal foster care from the FBI national crime databases.
    2) Amend federal law to help make it easier for states to provide criminal background check services to tribes that are licensing tribal foster homes. This access should allow tribes to not only submit requests to states to perform this service, but also allow tribes access to all criminal violations findings resulting from the background check.
    3) In coordination with tribes, work with BIA administrative officials to create a comprehensive training and technical assistance package to assist tribes in their knowledge and skills development to be able to successfully implement the Native Children's Safety Act requirements. The training and technical assistance should be provided through regular training sessions held throughout Indian Country and also by electronic resources, such as webinars and Internet-based resources.

Child Protection Programming in Indian Country

The need for effective child protection programs in tribal communities is significant, especially given high rates of at risk indicators that many tribal communities experience. Elevated levels of poverty, alcohol and substance abuse, and domestic violence can increase the risk for child abuse and neglect, especially in geographically isolated areas where often fewer services are available and many tribal communities reside. Access to state or county services in these rural areas are also less accessible and often are not well-equipped to effectively address the unique needs of tribal families and communities. Current data indicates that while Native children experience child abuse and neglect at an elevated rate, child neglect is by far the most commonly reported form of child maltreatment. State reported data on child maltreatment where Native children are involved indicates Native children are victims of child maltreatment at a rate of 13.8 per 1,000, the second highest rate for any racial or ethnic group, compared to the national rate of 9.2 children per 1,000 (Department of Health and Human Services, 2015).

All tribes provide some level of child abuse prevention and child protection services. These services may often be informal and include the use of extended family members or community elders, but they are an important partner to formal tribal child welfare program services. We sometimes describe how this natural helping system works as the more eyes and ears that you have in the community watching out for children the less likely you will have children experience maltreatment. Parents learn the expectations of the community in their role for helping keep children safe and benefit from those around them that support and guide them. This natural helping system came under attack several generations ago as Native children were forcibly separated from their families and tribes during the boarding school era and on into the 1950s through the 1970s with the Indian Adoption Project and Relocation era. These federal policies had disastrous effects upon generations of Native families destabilizing and disrupting the natural helping systems that once formed the core of child protection efforts in tribal communities.

Today, as tribes work to decolonize their communities and programs there is a resurgence of interest and movement to reinvigorate the natural helping systems within tribes and design child protection systems that are based upon community values and tribal culture. The success of these more contemporary efforts are seen in a number of tribes that have redesigned their programs to place less emphasis on doing primarily crisis services such as foster care and more to identify families at risk of abusing or neglecting their child early on before a full blown crisis ensues that requires removing the child and causing the family and child unnecessary trauma. In these tribal communities, we see outcomes that are beyond anything seen in other public child welfare systems. Foster care rates are reduced by as much as 70 percent and families are able to safely keep their children at home and avoid the revolving door that plagues many foster care systems in this country. These tribal models rely heavily on surrounding the family early on with support and having social workers that are appropriately trained and dedicated to intensive family engagement that works with the family in their unique cultural and social environment. All available supports, whether formal or informal, are actively utilized to help families succeed and keep children safe.

The ability to redesign a program from the inside using the community as your guide is open to all tribes, but the capacity to continue operating a program like the ones mentioned above happens because tribes have resources, ongoing sources of funding that can support this model of child safety. The examples in Indian Country are still promising and all have in common available tribal revenues that exceed most tribes. However, with additional federal support, like grant programs authorized under the Indian Child Protection and Family Violence Prevention Act, every tribe could potentially develop and operate this type of enhanced child protection programming. The child abuse prevention and treatment grant programs authorized under the Indian Child Protection and Family Violence Prevention Act are the only federal dedicated child abuse prevention and victim treatment funding for tribal governments, but have only been appropriated $5 million since 1990 when the law was enacted. Compare this to the $43 million of authorizations in the law for these critical grant programs which have never been funded. This is support that could help tribes develop much needed child abuse prevention and treatment services in their community, tribal programs that are similar to those mentioned earlier, and result in less trauma and uncertainty for tribal children and families. While the reforms of the Native American Children's Safety Act is an important move forward in ensuring child safety once they have been placed in foster care, appropriating grant funding under the Indian Child Protection and Family Violence Prevention Act is an opportunity to reduce the need to remove many Native children from their families in the first place.

Recommendations

1) Work with Congressional appropriations committees to support FY 2018 appropriations for the Indian Child Protection and Family Violence Prevention Act grant programs for tribes with special attention given to fully funding the Indian Child Abuse Treatment grant program ($10 million) and Indian Child Protection and Family Violence Prevention grant program ($30 million).

Conclusion

The First Kids 1st partner organizations greatly appreciate the efforts of Chairman Hoeven and Vice-Chairman Udall to hold this field hearing on efforts to protect Native children. Our organizations are involved in several different areas of work, but our common bond is our dedication to the well-being of Native children. No child can succeed in school or feel secure in their home or community if there aren't appropriate supports and protections in place to safeguard their well-being. The Native American Children's Safety Act helps by streamlining a number of the federal laws guiding criminal background checks for foster families licensed by tribes and improving safety for children by incorporating what is widely deemed as good practice in this process. The important next steps are to detangle and clarify the web of laws that govern tribal access to the national criminal databases administered by the FBI's Criminal Justice Information Center so every tribe can have easy and reliable access regardless of size, resources, and whether they want to work with a state or gain access directly. Furthermore, comprehensive and well-coordinated efforts to educate and train tribes about the requirements of the law are needed immediately. Lastly, we are seeing the great strides that tribes are making in increasing safety for their children and reducing the trauma for children and families that comes from over use of foster care. Investing in tribal child protection services and community-based resources with funding from the Indian Child Protection and Family Violence Prevention Act grant programs is key to increased child safety in Indian Country. As we are seeing in a number of successful tribal communities, there is no substitute for the kind of positive outcomes that can be found in tribal communities that have designed their child protection systems with culturally-based services that incorporate their unique community resources and approaches. This work is so important to our community's future and we greatly appreciate the opportunity to share our experience and knowledge in this area. As the Senate Committee on Indian Affairs continues their efforts to advance the well-being of our children and families we look forward to working closely with you.

RESPONSE TO WRITTEN QUESTIONS SUBMITTED BY HON. STEVE DAINES TO
MICHAEL S. BLACK

Question. As detailed in a December 2016 report published by the Montana Department of Justice Office of the Child and Family Ombudsman, tragically, 14 children died across Montana after reports of abuse were made to the Montana Department of Public Health and Human Services Child and Family Services Division. Of these 14 children, four were American Indian. Clearly, there is a strong need for better protections and care for Native American children in the foster care system. While the Native American Children's Safety Act is key to ensuring that tribal social services agencies can make informed decisions about child foster placements, what additional information, beyond the data points outlined in that Act, would benefit tribal social services agencies to have access to or be required to collect to enable tribes to better safeguard children in the foster care system?

Answer. Congress enacted the Native American Children's Safety Act (NACSA) on June 3, 2016. NASCA requires the Department of the Interior (DOI), Bureau of Indian Affairs (BIA) to issue guidance to Tribes on appropriate standards for foster-care placements by June 2018. The Assistant Secretary—Indian Affairs and B1A have partnered with the Department of Justice (DOJ), Federal Bureau of Investigation (FBI), and the Department of Health and Human Services, Administration for Children and Families to establish guidelines for Tribes to conduct: (1) a criminal records check, including a fingerprint-based check of national crime databases of all adults in any tribally ordered foster-care home; and (2) a check of Tribal and state abuse and neglect registries (this to include a check of all states where the individual has lived in the past 5 years) before a Tribe places an Indian child in foster care.

DOI's guidance will provide assurance, safeguards, and controls in the protection of Indian children when an out-of-home foster placement is necessary by the Tribe. To create a consistent and standard process, the AS–IA plan also includes offering training to Tribes on NACSA after finalization of the guidance.

What NACSA does not consider are two issues: access to information needed to conduct background checks, and resources needed to conduct background checks.

Many Tribes lack the resources to hire the staff needed to dedicate time to do the background checks, perform ongoing case management services, work on adjudications, and conduct the monthly site visits required by NACSA. Moreover, training on the various data systems used for background checks is needed. That is, Tribal social service programs need trained staff that is solely dedicated to working on the background checks, adjudicating and managing these cases, and conducting the monthly site visits required by NACSA.

Additionally, according to the Department of Justice, many Tribes have difficulty accessing the fingerprint-based criminal records check system for a variety of reasons. While both the Violence Against Women Act (VAWA) 2005 and Tribal Law and Order Act (TLOA) of 2010 provide authorization for tribal law enforcement agencies to access national crime information databases, tribal participation in national criminal justice information sharing depends upon state regulations, statutes, and policies in which tribal land is located. Tribes may face barriers to accessing and entering information into national crime information databases via state networks, so DOJ began the Tribal Access Program in 2015, which expands access to all national crime information databases to all authorized tribal civil and criminal justice agencies for tribes selected to participate in the program. Currently, 47 tribes either have or are in the process of obtaining a kiosk that provides access to the criminal records system through DOJ's Tribal Access Program (TAP). Additionally, although there are for-fee private organizations that provide this service, most of these services are prohibitively expensive.

Another barrier with regard to abuse and neglect records is that each state maintains its own closed registry of child abuse investigation records. That is, there is no one search engine that is capable of examining abuse and neglect records across multiple states. There is also no national child abuse registry for Tribes. In Indian country, many families have ties to other tribal communities. So, while Tribes can conduct background checks using their own court, law enforcement, or social service systems, they cannot search other tribal communities even though there may be relevant records there. This is challenging if a Tribe takes a hardline stance on confidentiality because NACSA does not require a search of other tribal child abuse registries. NACSA only requires Tribes to check state registries and its own tribal registries. Thus, the Bureau of Indian Affairs (BIA) plans to assist Indian Tribes in complying with NACSA by providing information on how to conduct background checks. The BIA has prepared a Draft NACSA Guidance document, entitled Background Checks For Foster Care Placements Under NACSA, for Tribes' review and comment. The Draft NACSA Guidance is also available at the following website: *https://www.bia.gov/as-ia/raca/regulations-and-other-documents-in-development*

During February 2018, the Office of the Assistant Secretary—Indian Affairs will be hosting Tribal consultation sessions to hear Tribes' input on this Draft NACSA Guidance.

————

RESPONSE TO WRITTEN QUESTIONS SUBMITTED BY HON. STEVE DAINES TO
NIKKI HATCH

Question. To ensure a child's foster care placement remains safe over time, what would you envision being key components of the recertification process required in the Native American Children's Safety Act?

Answer. The Native American Children's Safety Act, Public Law (P.L.) 114–165 directs the Department of the Interior (DOI) to issue guidance for Indian tribes to establish procedures to recertify homes or institutions in which foster care placements are made. The Department of Health and Human Services, Administration for Children and Families (ACF) is serving on a DOI working group for implementing P.L. 114–165. To begin these efforts, ACF is providing DOI assistance by helping them understand the similarities and differences in the requirements for foster homes and institutions under the title IV–E program and the provisions in this P.L. 114–165. For example:

- P.L. 114–165 requires that foster family homes and child care institutions are recertified periodically, including safety standards and background checks. Many title IV–E agencies voluntarily do so even though not required under title IV–E.

- Both P.L. 114–165 and title IV–E require child abuse and neglect registry checks and fingerprint-based checks of the National Crime Information Database (NCID) for prospective foster family homes and prohibit an individual from being approved if the individual has committed certain felonies. However, unlike title IV–E, P.L. 114–165 requires these criminal background checks for all individuals over age 18 residing in a foster family home or employed at an institution. [1]

- P.L. 114–165 exempts emergency foster care placements from the requirement that adult members of a foster family home and employees of institutions complete a fingerprint-based check of the National Crime Information Database (NCID) and that the tribe check to see if these individuals are on a state child abuse and neglect registry. Title IV–E does not allow agencies to claim IV–E foster care maintenance funds until the foster home or institution is licensed, which requires completion of all applicable background checks.

- P.L. 114–165 prohibits a foster care placement if an adult individual who resides in a foster family home or an employee of an institution is listed on a child abuse and neglect registry.

  —Title IV–E requires agencies to check or request a check of a child abuse and neglect registry for prospective foster families and adult members of the household, but allows the agency discretion in how to consider the results of the check and whether to approve the family.

  —Title IV–E does not require an NCID or child abuse and neglect registry check for every individual that is employed at a child care institution; rather it provides flexibility for the IV–E agency to have a process to provide for safety

———

[1] Note that title IV–B of the Social Security Act requires state agencies to ensure that all programs receiving IV–B funds require criminal background checks of all adults living in a prospective foster family home.

considerations of staff employed in institutions, which are often criminal background checks of employees in institutions.

○